What Is War?

Philosophical Reflections About the Nature, Causes, and Persistence of Wars

G. Lowell Tollefson

All Rights Reserved © 2007 by George Lowell Tollefson

ISBN-13: 978-0-9983498-6-2
ISBN-10: 0-9983498-6-0

Any resemblance to actual people and events in the fictional portion of this work is purely coincidental.

All rights reserved. No part of this book may be reproduced by any mechanical, photographic, or electronic process, or in the form of a phonographic recording; nor may it be stored in a retrieval system, transmitted or otherwise copied for public or private use (other than for "fair use" as brief quotations embodied in articles and reviews) without prior written permission.

Published by LLT Press, Eagle Nest, New Mexico
LLTPress.EagleNest@gmail.com

A special thanks to my wife, Loretta, for her long, patient years of support and tireless reading of manuscripts.

Table of Contents

What Is War? 1
The Attraction of War 4
The Problem with Civilians 9
Morality as Military Discipline 15
The Complexity of Counterinsurgent Operations 21
The Quality of Troops 27
Combat Deaths 33
The Rhythms of Conflict 39
Guerrilla Versus Counterinsurgent Operations 47
The Moral Uncertainty of War 53
The Socialization of Combat 60
War as a Reflection of Life 68
The Right of Military Interference 76
The Social Responsibility of Warring Nations 83
Discipline as a Military Virtue 90
The Fabrication of Wars 99
How War Defines Being 107
The Demands of War 115
The Many Historical Causes of War 122
Finding Purpose in the Military 133
The Ruthlessness of War 140
Military Power 147
A Veteran in Society 156
Good Logistics and Spiritual Fortitude 163
Casualties of War 170
Ordinary Men 178
Chapter Summary Questions 184
Sources and Recommended Reading 191

What Is War?

In any discussion of war, the question of its moral validity is apt to come up. Is there such a thing as a just war? If so, when should men resort to war as a means of settling differences? What kinds of differences produce wars, and what kinds of men fight them?

None of these questions are easy to answer because the standards by which we make moral decisions are themselves in question. For that reason, a discussion of war must include an examination of at least some of the fundamental principles of ethics. But any attempt to outline ethical issues must invariably take into consideration the social and psychological makeup of that curious creature we call man. Man—the creature we know best, since he is ourselves, and yet he's also the creature we know least. We know him least because he's too familiar. A subject is too close for observation when the observed and the observer are one and the same.

If we watch a bird preen, we're apt to assume it's cleaning and oiling its feathers. Others before us have noted that preening serves this function and doesn't tend to vary from a certain set pattern of behavior. So they've labeled it a form of instinctual behavior. The same is true of a dog turning around and around as it lies down. Well, we say, this behavior must be the result of an impulse of unremembered origin, in which the dog is attempting to smooth grasses to make a comfortable bed. The fact that there're no grasses present at the time of its turning is more than certain indication that the behavior is instinctual.

But when a woman suddenly starts pushing back her hair with both hands when an attractive man walks into her presence, thus displaying the outline of her breasts to best advantage, neither she nor we are apt to realize that this is probably the result of an instinctive impulse as well. The reason is that we're so close to the subject. We're talking about our own nature, and the little box of consciousness each of us lives in inclines us to believe that all our acts are indisputably free.

Thus the question of why a human being does what he or she does may not always be experimentally verifiable, since the person under observation can alter the grounds of the experiment when he's conscious of its purpose. If he isn't conscious of the experiment, he may be doing something entirely different from what the observer supposes, so the observer will have to ask him (or her) about his intentions, thereby informing him, at least to some extent, of the purpose of the experiment.

So an examination of our sociopolitical character as a species, and the further examination of our individual motives in any particular situation, are invariably fraught with difficulties. Yet these considerations must precede a discussion of war, especially if the discussion is to center upon its ethical merits or liabilities. By the time we get to the subject, we may well be exhausted. And it would seem that's generally been the case, because the philosophy of war is still very much an open subject.

Nevertheless, given the monumental importance of war in terms of its political consequences and in light of its often disastrous impact on the lives of so many human beings, we, or at least I in this case, feel compelled to give it another try. Some day, we may hope, one or two of us will hit upon some insight that will prove useful in understanding and perhaps even abolishing the phenomenon of war. Until that day arrives, even the most torturous foray into dark and unnavigable waters is probably worth the effort. Many missteps in a maze may eventually lead to a way out.

In each of the chapters that follow, the discussion is preceded by a vignette, a short fictional sketch giving a picture of one type of war, the American war that took place in Southeast Asia in the late 1960s and early 1970s. I played a role in that war as a United States Marine. Whatever the significance of my role, which was not great (I was enlisted), I've found the experience perplexing and unforgettable.

What Is War?

That's why I wrote the vignettes twelve years ago, after waiting nearly thirty years to broach the subject.

At first it was that particular war that troubled me and many other Americans. But in time I came to realize that all wars appear to exist in a moral vacuum. It's difficult to justify something so savage and inhumane as any war. Wars push human endurance and desperation to their utmost limits. They leave us spent, whether we're victors or losers. Yet few veterans can deny that their experience of it was not only unforgettable because of its horrors, but also because it left an indelible, bright spot in their memory which says, I was alive then in a way I never have been before or since.

What's the cause of this? Why do both nations and young people so often rush into war when it so often leads to ruin? In the chapters that follow, I've used the vignettes I wrote twelve years ago as a starting point of the discussion. They're only a starting point. This discussion is the product of twelve more years of thought.

The Attraction of War

The explosion was sudden, intense. I felt it more inside of me than outwardly. Then I became aware once again of the dust, heat and now of the smoldering jeep. The front end of it was twisted and it lay off the side of the road in a ditch. Beyond it the rice paddy. For some reason I was still on the road and John lay just a few feet away from me. I began to crawl over to him, feeling bruised and the sting of sweat in some cuts on my face.

"John," I called softly, becoming conscious of the fact that I was probably being watched, "you OK?" Raising myself cautiously on my arms, I saw his face, turned the other direction. The lower jaw was missing and the nearer side was a pulp. "John!" I lay on the warm road for several minutes.

Where were the damned VC? John's rifle was laying near him. I had no idea where mine was, where my weapon was. I carried a .45 caliber pistol. Crawling past John without looking at him again, I got the rifle, then rolled off into the ditch on the opposite side of the road from the jeep. It was just me and that wasn't going to last long. The earth was damp in the ditch from the rice field seepage. It felt cool. The road seemed to blaze above me in the hot sun. These dirt roads, so dusty and miserably hot. They were so easy to plant mines in. Where were the VC?

Lying there, I thought it over. These mine incidents on Liberty road were almost always followed by an ambush. Yet there had been no small arms fire. No one had yet appeared out of the dense brush, the copses of trees surrounding the rice paddies on both sides of the road. I was nearly a mile from the nearest firebase, the battalion command post. I knew they had probably heard the explosion.

What Is War?

I began to crawl along the ditch. It was then I thought I heard voices. But then I wasn't sure. I heard them again. I crawled as quickly as I could without raising my profile above the edge of the road. I knew it was stupid to try to get away and my heart was pounding so hard I couldn't hear the voices above it now. It would be easier crawling without the rifle and I'd be outnumbered anyway, but I clung to its cold plastic and metal as if it were a lover. It wasn't the thought of using it now, it was just the thought of not having it, of not having anything.

I became exhausted after several minutes and stopped moving. Now I could hear the voices again and they were definitely Vietnamese. No one would mistake Vietnamese sounds for English. I tried to raise my head just enough to see. Three of them, one female. One man had khakis on. The other looked like he was wearing an American jungle utility uniform. He was carrying an American rifle. The woman, or girl, had a carbine slung over her left shoulder. She wore the white cotton blouse and black silk pajama bottoms of a peasant. The legs were rolled up to her thighs, as if she'd just come from planting rice in a field. They were standing over John. The man in khakis walked over to the jeep and then back. He said something and they all began looking in various directions down the road and over the fields.

They're searching for me, I thought. How was it they hadn't seen me? Quietly, very slowly I pulled back the rifle bolt, released it and pushed the charging handle into place. A bullet popped out of the chamber. I knew John should have already had the weapon cocked, but I wasn't sure. I pushed the selector to automatic fire.

But I didn't fire. I was clearly within range but was afraid. There might be others and I'd be overwhelmed.

I waited and waited. They quit looking around and went on talking. The man in American uniform knelt down and started searching John's body. Obviously he was experienced at this. Because John's body was twisted at 180 degrees, the head came over when the man turned the body. The grisly face made me sick but I noticed the girl did not even react, and she was so young.

Then I heard the sound of a vehicle, the sound of more than one. Marines were coming from the command post to check things out. The VC searching John's body got up startled and they all started talking rapidly. That's when I opened fire, emptying the magazine in my rifle. Nineteen rounds. The three of them fell in a heap.

As the first vehicle, a small utility truck, came into sight around a bend in the road, I got up and started walking carefully toward the tangle of bodies around John. I loaded another magazine into my rifle as I walked and wiped the sweat and dust off my forehead with my arm.

* * *

War is cruel. Yet men seek it out. These are mostly young men without commitment to family and career. What draws them?

The fact that war is cruel doesn't seem to act as a deterrent. Fear isn't a significant factor within the safety of imagination. It's only when the combatant is faced with real danger that the fear is felt with sufficient force to be daunting. Yet how many former combatants remember their war experiences with an emotion that can only be called affection, in spite of hard memories? Clearly, there's something about the war experience that transcends both fear and horror.

Can we say that war is beautiful? There's a sense in which it is so. But one might suggest what a terrible thing it must be to find beauty in suffering and destruction. Why is it beautiful? Why is seeing a companion's face blown half off both traumatic and unforgettable? Isn't it strange that killing is made acceptable in this context, yet many veterans of combat avoid violence throughout the remainder of their lives?

My experiences as a Marine in Vietnam were not so terrible as some, yet my memory of the war was searing, even somewhat debilitating for some time. In spite of this, I know I wouldn't change my course of action if I had it to do over again.

If war is ever to be eliminated, some questions must be asked. This is the first one: What need in human nature is supplied by such an experience? And what could be made to substitute for it?

To begin, we must consider that there's a paradoxical experience of cleanliness in war. What do I mean by cleanliness? Certainly not battlefield conditions. What I mean would come closer to being described as a cleanliness of soul. Here again I'm not referring to the emotional turmoil, horror, guilt, and trauma that is felt. Or am I? Beyond these emotions, yet inextricably bound up with them, is something else. It's a kind of purgation, or coming through.

From birth every human being grows in his or her sense of personal limitation. We learn of death. We experience denial and privation. We see this cause of suffering in all who surround us. In essence, we're bugs in a carpet tread upon endlessly by heavy boots. Out of this comes a feeling of suffocating being, in which there's no remittance, except that of final limitation, or ceasing to exist.

Then there is war. It comes as a release to the strong, young heart which says, "I'll go and have a look at the final boundaries of things. When I return (this is always a matter of faith in the young), I'll know that I've been larger than my circumstances. I will have come through."

That is the draw of war. It's a confrontation with reality. It's a pitting of the soul—immaterial and uncompromising—against the physical forces of limitation. We learn of physical limitation every moment of our lives, but as simple conscious beings we perceive ourselves as unlimited. We're mind and spirit, and spirit is free. One of these two interpretations must give way to the other. A strong heart chooses freedom.

But if this was all there were to it, extreme sports might supply a simpler solution. War provides something more. It supplies community of purpose in braving limitation. Men join military organizations and go to war in fighting units. It's in this way that war changes every life that's touched by it. It sears each heart with a brand by giving it a depth of communal understanding. The experience was shared, not solitary, and there was a mutual dependence and cooperation in it. Those who've been through war live together on other soil than that of those who haven't. To some extent, even the fortunes of the enemy, or those of any noncombatants who were present in the zone of combat, become part of this communal feeling.

If we're to get rid of war, we must give humanity, particularly our idealistic youth, not only a greater sense of common interest, but a spirit of transcendence as well. How can this be done in a bitter world of venal trivialities devoted to physical comfort and emotional complacence? Civilizations such as ours are weakened by the loss of their best, their most vigorous and daring, people in war. But these civilizations lose them because they are weak in themselves. Until we learn how to build a vigorous, life-affirming and life-transcending world, alienation and war will always be the favored options—especially for the young and as yet undefeated in heart.

What Is War?

The Problem with Civilians

When I arrived for the first time at the firebase on hill 55 and was still new in Vietnam, I saw my first USO show. It wasn't much. The Marines there had built a small wooden platform and the performers, several men and women who were comedians and singers, four people in all, were using it as a stage. They had arrived by helicopter and were working through their act when I got there. But they were so nervous their performance wasn't very good.

They weren't doing well because there was a firefight in progress somewhere off the south side of the hill. You couldn't see much because of the thick brush jungle near the bottom of the hill. But the gunfire was steady and automatic and there were occasional shouts. While this was going on there were Marines sitting all over the tops of tanks and amphibious vehicles parked in a ring that went completely around the stage. They were wearing flack jackets and helmets, had M-16 rifles, grenade launchers and machine guns and were covered with belts of ammunition which were slung over their chests and shoulders. But they weren't interested in the firefight, the racket and commotion. That was a problem for the unlucky squad that wasn't on top of the hill watching the show with them. The shooting finally ended, and I think when the choppers took out our guests they were more than happy to go.

I was brand new and trained as an interpreter, so right away they had a use for me. A dirt road ran straight through our compound. It was a major transportation route. An old woman had come to one of our checkpoints and wanted to pass on through. I went down to interpret and saw that she was carrying a split bamboo pole loaded with straw baskets. Heavy too. She was bent over and wrinkled but had that endurance and strength Vietnamese peasants always seemed to have. She said she wanted to go to market in a nearby village down the road. I told the sentry I'd take her through. Since I was a non-commissioned officer and he was a lower rank, he figured I knew what I was doing and let her go.

Well, I didn't. I had no idea about these people. We walked along, the old woman trudging very slowly under her load. Believe me, that pole was heavy! I tried it. I don't know what those baskets were loaded with but they weighed a ton and the pole's sharp edges cut into my shoulder. As we walked, she kept looking all around. Just curious, I thought. But a week later we were hit at night with a sapper attack. We fought them off but they managed to plant a plastic explosive charge on every listening or observation post bunker we had on the west side of the hill, as well as on our bridge down below. They knew where everything was, thanks to that old woman. They even broke through our perimeter wire at one place and killed six Marines, wounding twelve. We never knew what their casualties were, but at least they didn't have time to set off any of the plastic explosives they'd planted.

The worst part was knowing what I'd done. But I never told anybody. Not for a long time anyway. Finally one night I opened up. The lieutenant and I were walking the perimeter line at dusk, distributing ammunition and helping to set up claymore mines for the night perimeter guard.

As we walked from one bunker to another, I said, "I killed those guys."

"What are you talking about, sergeant?" The lieutenant was a very tall, thin faced looking guy, whose brown eyes would get big when he was excited or confused. It made you laugh sometimes.

"Those seven Marines, sir." Another one had died after the wounded were taken out by helicopter for medevac.

"You mean, sergeant, you were running around on the outside of the perimeter shooting at them?"

"No, that's not what I meant, sir." Why was I bothering?

What Is War?

"I don't understand you, sergeant."

"It's nothing, sir."

"What do you mean nothing?"

"I was just talking."

"Those guys over there need ammo. And you'd better show them how to set up their claymore. They leave it like that, they're going to blow their own faces off."

"Aye aye, sir."

After my tour of duty was over and I was back in the States, having learned a little more, it still bothered me sometimes. Like that nervous USO troop I saw, I was still trying to make sense out of what was going on. Both here in America and over in Vietnam. I thought of the lieutenant sometimes. He had been transferred to another assignment several months into my tour over there. They often did that with officers. Well, I had heard later that he'd led a patrol into an ambush that should've been obvious to him and had lost some of his men. It was a stupid thing that he did, and any one of those guys he was leading could have warned him. But he was the lieutenant and I guess they figured he knew what he was doing.

* * *

Like most human activities, war isn't a perfected art. Neither the lieutenant nor the sergeant here are perfect. They're caught in the confusion that is war, and it's the objective of the insurgent fighter to add to this confusion. In this particular case, and that of the lieutenant later, the insurgents were successful. But war in general, and particularly a guerrilla war, is a series of plans, misapprehensions, mistakes and the final triumph of those who endure.

When I speak of those who endure, I'm speaking only of the triumph of spirit. America didn't win its objectives in Vietnam, but this doesn't mean the Americans on the ground failed. The Marines I knew never lost their faith in the Corps. They did what had to be done. Though professional in performance, they made mistakes, as all soldiers do. But those mistakes, by the standards of armed conflict, were not many. Ironically, along with the U.S. Army and the other American armed forces, they went on to win most of their direct engagements with the enemy, yet lost the war.

Since success in suppressing a guerilla insurgency can be elusive and depends on outside factors, such as the willingness of a nation to support such an effort, the question might be asked, What's permissible, or ethical, in pursuing a military objective? It's a hard question. The nature of insurgent warfare is to wear down a superior opponent by denying him decisive contests on open ground. Unfortunately, this includes making use of civilian populations for concealment and deception. The use of civilians places them under suspicion and puts them in the line of fire. So how does one treat a population that's often perceived as untrustworthy?

There's no simple answer because war is by its nature an abandonment of standards and agreements. There's no ethical basis for war. All civility is gone. However, that doesn't mean that troops should be undisciplined or cruel in their treatment of a civilian population. Innocence is innocence in any context and should be treated with humanity. But where is the innocence in this incident? The old woman is furthering the objectives of the enemy. She's actively taking sides. Did she choose to do this, or was she coerced? It would be hard to determine. But the sergeant's mistake (the sergeant being new to the conflict) was to assume her innocence. *He* was the innocent party, and, in being so, he inadvertently let down his comrades.

Perhaps (overlooking the sergeant's jaundiced point of view born of guilt and resentment) the lieutenant later did the same sort of thing. He made a wrong assumption. It's easy to say the ambush could've been avoided, when it's no longer possible to change the outcome. Both men were caught in circumstances so alien to their frank and open upbringing that their adjustment was rendered costly to themselves and others.

So again, what is morality in war? We've already said there's no ethical basis for it. So to answer this question, we must ask what morality is. It would be nice to assume it was carved in stone by a supernatural power. Perhaps it has been. Perhaps there are revelations concerning human conduct that are eternally true. But in practice the rules and norms of every society go far beyond a universal standard. This is evidenced by all the variation to be found across the world.

Such variations are the product of environment and economic structure. They have to do with where we live and how we divide up the task of living together in a community. How much more varied and restricted might those rules be in a war, where the community has been narrowed and the task severely focused? In other words, where the principal objective is restricted to preserving the lives of oneself and one's comrades (if possible) while carrying out a mission to destroy an enemy.

Yet there's something more universal than a consideration of a physical and social environment and its economic structure. It demands human allegiance even in war, the most elemental and cruel of circumstances. It is that there must be an environment of trust between individuals who would act and live, even fight and possibly die, together. That's the bond of community, especially of every combat soldier with every other in the same uniform. It's what is usually written in scripture, or stone, for social purposes. It's also what decency, or an empathetic character, would demand of anything resembling a human level of mutual participation, awareness, and understanding.

On the one hand, the enjoyment of any suffering imposed upon the innocent is an abomination to all. But, on the other, innocence cannot be attributed to an opponent on the battlefield since, if he hopes to prevail, he must seize every advantage that comes within his means, and that includes deception. After all, his purpose is to destroy *his* opponent.

So, what about civilians? In guerrilla warfare, where the civilian population is inevitably exploited and some of its members are discovered to be engaged in aiding and abetting the enemy, the rule of empathy is frequently abridged. Some people are innocent and deserving of a respect for their lives and property, for which they must trust and for which they are helplessly dependent upon those who possess the means of their destruction, while others are all but uniformed combatants themselves. And in most cases, one can't be distinguished from the other.

There can only be one approach to this dilemma: the exercise of cautious discipline. Yet such is the nature of war that men are sometimes pushed beyond their endurance when they see their friends killed by those they can't trust. This grievance is further aggravated by the fact that in insurgent warfare, these same men are frequently denied an open settlement of accounts with the enemy. All their pain is resolved in frustration and anger. This is why discipline becomes a rule, not only of a commitment to one another and to a mission in combat, but of a cautious restraint when dealing with matters unrelated to these goals. It's not easy to exercise.

Morality as Military Discipline

In the old French building some of the tiles were missing from the roof. In fact, half the roof was gone. Still, we used to sleep in there. Most of the time the hole in the roof didn't matter, and during the rainy season we would shelter ourselves as best we could under the tiles that remained. It was better than the bunkers.

This building was in the center of a small hamlet that lined a dirt road. Not much to look at but the road was considered important. So our nine man patrol was permanently assigned there to guard the village. We did supposedly have some help but it was hard to tell how much. A couple dozen Popular Forces soldiers were assigned to reinforce us. But we never saw all of them and few of them were reliable. During the day they were usually out on work projects for the District Chief.

Once, when we were hit at night by the VC, we had eight of them with us. They were strung out along the three bunkers we had facing the open field and distant tree line west of the village.

I was asleep when the shooting started. No mortars. Just rifle fire coming from the tree line. You have to be a good shot to hit anything at that distance in the dark—close to six hundred yards—but they were doing all right. You could hear some of the rounds thudding into the sandbags and the rest of them whistling faintly overhead. I had three of these Popular Forces guys with me. Two of them were on watch. The other one and myself were asleep. It was our four hour rest break.

We were all on top of the bunker because it was the rainy season and the inside, which was dug part way into the ground, was always wet. We had an M-60 machine gun. The two guys on watch were

Tollefson

having trouble getting the ammunition belt to feed into the gun and it kept jamming, so I got up, pulled the belt out, emptied the chamber, put the belt back in place and closed the cover. One of the soldiers started firing while I held the belt up and carefully fed it to the gun.

I don't think there is anything more beautiful than the way tracers arc at night, as long as they aren't coming toward you. They seem almost to float, to sail in a leisurely way toward their destination.

Once we got the machine gun going the firing stopped, the shooting that was coming from the tree line. Even though our other two bunkers were also answering their fire, the VC didn't stop until we opened up with the only machine gun. Six hundred yards is really too far for sighting in with an M-16.

"They come back," the Popular Forces soldier said, releasing the trigger. He wiped his face with his sleeve. The other two soldiers were silent. I could feel as well as see their worry.

Maybe they will come back, maybe not, I thought. "Depends on how many are out there," I said.

"They come back," the soldier said.

Two Marines climbed onto the bunker. Steve and Roger. Roger, a sergeant, was our squad leader. They had been sleeping in the French building.

I don't know how the Viet Cong did it. It was maybe a half hour when all of a sudden we started catching fire from the village. The village! That was behind us and now they opened up at the tree line again. I started firing my M-16 at the tree line, lying as flat as I could. We had a small parapet of sandbags built up on that side but nothing on the other.

Men on the other two bunkers were firing in both directions. The PF I had helped with the machine gun was lying beside me, shooting carefully at muzzle flashes with his carbine.

Roger was swearing the way he always did when he was upset. He stood up and turned the machine gun around toward the village. Screaming at one of the other PFs, he got him to feed the belt to the gun. Steve was using his M-16, shooting toward the village. The VC had set fire to a couple of buildings. One of them was our French building. You could see human shapes moving about among the flames.

"Goddamn!" I said. There were several figures moving toward us out of the tree line. I saw them run zigzag into the field and hit the ground. I began to imagine one of the things I feared most: if we weren't all killed, we'd be captured.

That's when I noticed him. The other PF. I had turned to tell Roger what was happening and caught sight of him running. He veered at an angle, going toward the village but into the dark away from all the activity. I saw a couple more PFs running from the other bunkers.

"Don't let them get away!" Roger shouted. Steve shifted the barrel of his rifle to the right and fired. The PF spun half way around and fell to the ground. But he got back up, holding his arm, and stumbling into a run, kept on going.

"I should have told you to kill him," Roger said.

The machine gun had cleared the activity out of the village, so Roger turned it back toward the tree line. Steve crawled over to my left side. The PF helping Roger continued feeding the belt. I'm not sure what the other one was doing. I think he was watching the village.

It was hard to see in the dark by only the light of the tracers, but we thought we saw several figures run back into the tree line. Shortly after that the shooting stopped. Everything stopped.

In the morning we found our building a little charred but still usable. Some canteens, ammunition and a flack jacket were gone. But there weren't any bodies. I don't know about that damned PF or the others who ran off. We never saw any of them again.

* * *

The three cardinal virtues of a military ground unit are discipline, esprit de corps, and unit integrity. They're intertwined and inseparable. Discipline builds spirit, a commitment to the military organization of which you are a part. And spirit creates unit integrity, which is born of the mutual commitment of the members of the unit to each other. Good military training emphasizes all three. The Marine Corps develops each of these virtues, both together and individually. It's always an issue. It's been said that a Marine going into combat often fears disgracing or letting down his Corps and his unit more than the possibility of death.

It's possible for purposes of discussion to reduce these three elements to one. This is because esprit de corps and unit integrity can only arise out of an unshakable habit of discipline, a willingness to obey orders and carry out a mission immediately without questioning. The important element here is trust. That's the building block of all three, especially discipline. But trust, we've said before, is the core, heart-centered condition underlying the establishment of moral relations. It's what any community, civilian or military, is built upon.

When military training is carried out, it must create a bond of reliance in the hearts of those trained. That reliance is the belief that the military organization, the unit, and the comrade under arms—these being, in a sense, one and the same—can be trusted absolutely with one's life and the common mission. In the Marine Corps this creates a mutual respect at all levels of rank and sometimes a contempt for those who don't appear to possess these virtues. This respect is not always expressed in a warmhearted way. It's rough, uncompromising, and genuine.

The question that arises for philosophical consideration is the question of the moral bond. How does that compare to the moral bond in civilian life (a civil setting), and how does it differ? Remembering that two things apply to any moral setting—first, the physical and economic and, second but more importantly, the need for trusting relationships—we can examine how each, the civil and the military, works.

In a civil community trust runs broadly through a number of situations, such as the right to hold property, the need for personal safety, and freedom to act within and participate in the community.

But it doesn't run deep. There's generally no life and death situation here. If there was, it would most likely be a condition of war. The commitment of one citizen to another is casual. Certainly in a sound community they should work to promote the good of one another, but that good is remote.

The effects of one's actions upon another are often not immediately discernible. A citizen goes about his business, seeing to his private concerns, and taking care only that his acts don't interfere with those of another. Much of what we trust in as individuals in a civil setting is to be left alone, except where the general interests of the community are concerned.

Not so the military. Here trust is a matter of life and death, and any neglect on the part a combatant in performing his duties has an immediate impact on the lives of his comrades and the success and reputation of his unit. This bond of trust isn't so broad. There're fewer concerns, especially in combat where personal needs are fewer and the communal need is greater. For this reason, the bond is one of affection and immediate mutual concern, rather than one of laissez faire, or noninterference in the affairs of others. It's narrow, but the emotion runs deep. Thus, at least in one sense, it's the opposite of the civil bond. Interest, not tolerance, is its kindling flame.

This interest is much of the appeal of military service. It's an ideal condition in which each member of the community is committed to the others with body, heart, and mind. There are differences, but they're not the differences of indifference. They're differences struck off as sparks in the heat of close association—differences in determining how to interpret the mutual interest. Without a rigorous discipline, such differences might cause harm. But in a welded body of troops they rarely do.

The physical and economic component of moral relations in a civil community is that which establishes laws and norms of behavior. It gives the precise character to these rules, and these rules are the component that differs in societies across the world. A modern, democratic society in a temperate climate and fertile region won't have the same attitudes and rules as a medieval society in a desert. Still, a civil bond of trust will exist in each of them in some form, expressed according to the prevailing rules.

The physical and economic component of the military is different. It determines, not the rules of relations, but those of strategy and tactics. A well funded, armament enriched military will seek conventional engagements where possible, so that it can put its material advantages to work. A military lacking these things will seek unconventional methods of engagement to protect it from the unequal use of arms.

Thus it appears that what was the physical and economic component of morality *within* a civil community is inapplicable in a moral sense to a relationship *between* opposing forces. It becomes an expedient relationship between those forces, because in the open field of conflict there's no real question of trust. In this way, physical and economic factors apply to the relations between opposing forces but not to the relations of individuals within each force. The physical and economic are therefore not really a component of morality insofar as the military is concerned.

I've engaged in this discussion to point out what makes the military experience unique and attractive to spirited individuals. Here the divisive considerations of material advantage and circumstance are excluded from the conditions of a moral relationship. All that remains inside the military environment, all that pertains to the manner in which men of war support, aid, and trust one another is a simple, close, and uniform relation of trust. That's the condition of morality in its purest form. As such it's profoundly appealing to the quickened heart, enlarged imagination, and innate optimism of the young. It's a superior condition which, once tasted, is long treasured in memory.

What Is War?

The Complexity of Counterinsurgent Operations

We entered the village near dawn, at the first full light of day. It wasn't very big, just a small hamlet tucked into the brush jungle of the lowland country. It wasn't even near a road. But it was considered heavily fortified and under Viet Cong control. That's what made it important.

I was one of the first people in, riding on top of a tank with the first squad of the second platoon. As we rolled into the village from an open field on its south end, the Vietnamese were gathered together in a group at its center with huts on either side. The whole crowd backed up together as we came slowly toward them.

The tank stopped. Sgt. Derek ordered his men to dismount and sent a fire team along the row of huts on either side. The second and third squads had deployed on the outer perimeter of the village, to the east and west, and were closing in together on the north end. This village had created a lot of problems and we were going to flush the Viet Cong out.

In a few minutes the two fire team leaders returned and one of them reported to Sgt. Derek that he had found a small cache of weapons in a hut. The villagers who were gathered before us continued standing there looking at us. We looked at them. How do you pick out a Viet Cong or a sympathizer, especially from a bunch of women, old men and children? There weren't any young men anywhere. There never were.

"Where are the VC?" I asked in Vietnamese. I had come along for that purpose. They all just looked at me.

"We won't harm you if you tell us where they went," I said. "Don't be afraid."

No one said anything. Sgt. Derek looked wearily along either row of huts. This clustered silence was the usual procedure. Whether they were afraid to answer or didn't want to was hard to tell.

"Get on the tank," he said.

"You going to burn it?" the tank commander asked, sticking his head and shoulders out of the hatch above the turret. The platoon leader, a young lieutenant who was now with one of the other two squads, had given Sgt. Derek the authority to make that decision.

"I don't know." He turned to the fire team leader who'd found the weapons cache. This guy was an Alaskan Indian whose left hand was badly scarred. He had been wounded by an explosive charge left behind at an observation post a week before he'd occupied it. That bunker had been overrun by Communist sappers, or combat engineers, who had planted the charge. The Indian's name was Mike, Corporal Mike we usually called him.

"What do you think, Mike?"

"Marines have been fired on from this village. We've got every right. Especially since they won't talk."

In the front of the crowd I could see one woman whose face was thickly pockmarked. I had been studying her for several minutes thinking she had the worst case of acne I'd ever seen. Now it suddenly dawned on me that her face was full of tiny bits of shrapnel. She held a small child about a year old. It didn't look very healthy, though the breast she was feeding it certainly was ample.

Now we were all looking at them. Two very different groups of people trying to figure each other out.

"Let's go," Sgt. Derek said. All the men in the squad had returned from the search. A couple were carrying the few weapons they'd found in the cache: a Russian AK-47 and a couple of Chinese carbines.

The tank screeched and groaned backwards out of the village with its ninety millimeter gun still pointing at the small crowd of Vietnamese.

What Is War?

Two days later another patrol was sent into the village to burn it.

* * *

The squad leader in this incident didn't exercise the decision making authority that had been given to him. Two days later a patrol was sent in to burn the village. Since weapons had been found and previously much hostile activity had come from the village, there could be little doubt there was an enemy presence there and that the villagers were well acquainted with it. Yet the squad leader's reaction raises a fundamental issue: It's more difficult to look an enemy in the eye and carry out hostile action against him, especially if the enemy appears to be unarmed and you're not sure it's the enemy.

War then can be conducted in two ways. It can be carried out from a distance where there's no personal contact between antagonists. Or it can be waged close up, where contact is possible, even certain at times. Most infantrymen do their killing from a distance of at least a grenade throw, but at times it's done with bayonets and hand to hand. This is close and nasty, but there's no time for reflection. It's kill or be killed.

But what happens when apparently unarmed civilians are involved and you're almost, but not quite, certain they're hostile? You see them close enough to witness their vulnerability, and you have time to discover their humanness and suffering. The anger, fear, and excitement of combat are momentarily settled into your background of feeling. To act then might be cruelty rather than expediency. That was the squad leader's dilemma.

Sgt. Derek could've made his decision to destroy the village with a clear conscience, at least from a military point of view. He had every reason to punish the villagers. They were harboring the enemy. That enemy had killed and wounded his fellow Marines. But it was also true that the enemy was armed; the villagers weren't. How willing was their aid? If it was given freely, then how many of the villagers were involved and how many weren't? Should the innocent and the weak suffer together with the guilty?

That the decision was finally made to destroy the village, in spite of Sgt. Derek's hesitation, is possibly an indication that a cooler head saw the tactical necessity of it. But it may just as well have been that the decision maker, being less intimately involved with those who would be affected by his decision and more immediately aware of previous losses, simply followed his own impulse as surely as the sergeant had. That decision maker may have been the lieutenant or someone above him.

Strange to say, or perhaps not so strange, there were no Viet Cong or NVA (North Vietnamese Army soldiers) present in the village at the time of the sweep. Whatever harm was done wouldn't have directly affected them, unless they'd left loved ones in the village, which was unlikely.

This is the fundamental inhumanity of insurgent operations. By involving the civilian populace in varying degrees, both willing and unwilling, the insurgents create a gray area of cover for their own tactical moves. It's not just a matter of identification, of not knowing who or where the insurgents are. More importantly, it's a matter of culpability. Who's to blame, and for how much? Are the civilians insurgents themselves, passive sympathizers, or merely coerced?

An angry response on the part of the Marines could do more harm than good, since winning over the populace is an important part of winning this type of war. The guerillas depend upon the local farmers to supply them with necessities and allow them to move about undetected. The local people also provide recruits. Winning them over could strangle the guerilla movement.

But leaving a nest of insurgents operating on one's flank and rear is also unwise. A quick decision must be made where more time and more thorough knowledge might render the decision wrong. This is why guerilla wars are so hard to fight. Moral confusion becomes a weapon in the hands of the insurgents.

What Is War?

Create moral ambiguity for the enemy forces, and they'll falter. They'll either overreact or underreact. Most likely the loss of comrades will cause an overreaction. The local populace will be alienated, sweep operations will become even more difficult for those combating the insurgents, and insurgent strongholds will increase in size and number, providing more flexibility for guerilla strikes.

Philosophically, the question is this: In such an atmosphere of uncertainty, what is not only tactical and expedient, but what is ethically a sound approach? Can military operations be carried out in such an environment without inflicting heavy casualties on innocent civilians? By most accounts, civilian casualties in Vietnam were very high. This seems to have been the result of too aggressive a policy of search and destroy—that is, taking the war to the enemy and ignoring the populace. Some search and destroy would certainly have been necessary, but winning over the populace and securing areas of the country against guerilla infestation might've consolidated gains and saved innocent lives.

This approach might've been ethically sounder and tactically firmer. It was the approach originally employed by the Marine Corps in Vietnam, as it had been in Central America, but it was overridden by higher command, General Westmoreland himself. Since the war wasn't won, the question of which approach was better may never be answered. (Would it have been answered if the war *had* been won?) But ethically it might be asked, Is any war in which the population can't be won over a war that should be fought?

If the populace is all in support of the insurgency or divided between that and indifference, leaving little affirmative support for outside interference, then any military campaign mounted in opposition to the insurgency is simply an invasion of the country and a usurpation of that country's locally constituted power. It might be that the true will of the people isn't based in the capital but is reflected in the insurgency. If so, it should be left to those people to work out their national destiny.

To come to the aid of a corrupt and unpopular government is to invade the country in which it resides. This is what our own American declaration of independence implies when it states that the people have a right to dissolve the bands of government when that government no longer represents their interests. If a nation acts against its own stated principles of sovereignty in interfering in the affairs of another nation, then it has by its own admission perpetrated an act of war against that nation.

But the problem is this: How does one determine what the will of a people is? A large portion of any population just wants to get on with the business of daily living and would choose whatever side could guarantee peace. Furthermore, is there such a thing as the will of a people? Wasn't the will of the people at the end of the American Revolution simply the will of the victors, as opposed to that of the opposition and the indifferent middle?

This is where the complexity of counterinsurgent operations lies. There's no solid moral basis for a foreign power putting down an insurgency in another country at the request of its possibly unpopular government, especially if the interfering power insists on representing principles of popular sovereignty. Furthermore, conducting such a war anywhere is a morally hazardous business, since innocents in large numbers must inevitably get into the line of fire. And yet none of this touches upon the essential moral ambiguity of war itself. It's in addition to it.

The Quality of Troops

The sound of women keening. I've heard it before but not like that. It sounded like only a few voices, yet it was loud and could be heard above the rumble and creaking of the tank. There had just been a firefight in the village not more than an hour before. One of our patrols had encountered heavy Viet Cong resistance where they had least expected it, and they'd taken some casualties without being able to dislodge the VC. So they'd pulled back, surrounded the village and called for us on the radio.

When we got there, there was still an exchange of small arms fire going on, but it was light. The second and third squads had orders to enter the village from the south while firing on it from the west, then the first squad would approach from the northwest. A small river bounded the village on the east. That meant the Viet Cong would try to escape north, and that's what we wanted them to do.

An M-48 tank is not a comfortable way to travel. It's crowded inside, and everything you land on, when going into a hole or climbing out of one, is hard. It carries a ninety millimeter main gun and a thirty caliber machine gun at the tank commander's hatch in the turret. There are four crewmen. The driver is up front and below. That way, if he takes the tank over any mines, he's the first to know about it. That was my job. The gunner and the loader are in the main body of the tank, right behind and a little above the driver. They have just enough room to do their job.

As we approached the village through a rice paddy from the south, we could see movement on the village street just behind the two nearest huts. The tank commander relayed that information over his radio headset. We were slipping in the mud that was beneath the shallow water of the rice paddy. I felt the right track slip, and that caused us to veer suddenly to the right.

"Damn!" I said. We'd been stuck before and I didn't want that to happen now.

"Slow it down, Walt! Let it grip," the tank commander yelled.

We continued toward the village at a crawl. Someone opened up to the right of us and a red string of tracer bullets hit the thatch roof of one of the nearest huts and started it burning. At first you could just make out a little gray wisp of smoke, but then you could see the flames. In the background some figures were moving. There were four or five. One of them stopped and fired before all of them disappeared behind a hut three or four huts back. But there were more of them. A solid wall of fire opened up, most of it directed toward the Marines who had fired the burst of tracers from our right. All the while, as we approached, there had been keening, but now it stopped.

We moved slowly forward. The ninety millimeter gun swung around and lowered itself over my head. I heard my tank commander giving orders to the gunner but couldn't hear clearly enough to make out what they were. I knew anyway. That's why the gun and the tank were both pointed in the same direction.

The eeriest moment in a situation like this is when there's a lull, when all the shooting stops and there's just the radio chatter. Just the radio chatter and the creaking of the tank treads in the sloshy water, the diesel engine barely humming. Then the gun went off, the tank rocking backward while still moving forward, and you could see the round going. It was a heat round, high explosive, and the hut it hit, several hooches back where we'd seen the four or five VC, simply collapsed. It blew outward in a cloud of dust and fell in a heap. If there was anybody in or behind it, they were just corpses now.

"Hold it, Walt!"

I stopped the tank. The Marines to the west of the village opened up with heavy fire, and I could now see figures coming out of hooches and running down the village street toward the north. There were *holes for cover and bunkers in those huts. The figures trying to get out were armed. The rest of the people remained in the holes.*

The Marines to my right were moving forward, firing, running short distances in a leapfrog fashion. There were still VC in some of the huts because they kept up heavy fire both to the south and west. We just sat there. The first squad had worked its way around from the northwest to the north of the village and to fire now would endanger them. Our job was done anyway. We had flushed out some of the VC.

Our infantry still took casualties. There was no small number of VC in the village. But their losses were greater, and I don't think any of them got away.

The infantry rounded up the people in the middle of the village street. They searched all the hooches, then burned them. Pajama clad bodies were everywhere, along the village street, on the road to the north and in the rice field beside it, with their weapons scattered around them.

Standing there in the middle of the burning village, surrounded by black smoke and flames, were silent staring faces, half of them kids covered with dirt and frightened, and three or four women keening. Probably the ones we'd heard before.

* * *

We've spoken of the Viet Cong penchant for concealment among the populace. But this isn't an occasionally occupied hamlet. It's fortified. Whatever measure of coercion might've been used on some of the people, it's necessary to assume that most of those here are hardened supporters of the Viet Cong. Given the time period (1967–68) and place (Quang Nam province) about which these vignettes were written, the Viet Cong ranks were probably filled with North Vietnamese Army regulars.

Each of the vignettes, as we go through them, is like a snapshot of general events in Quang Nam province at the time. During this period, I was assigned for six and a half months as a Vietnamese interpreter with the 3rd Battalion of the 7th Marine Regiment in the 1st Marine Division. I was part of Headquarters and Service Company, which occupied the battalion command post located at a firebase on hill 37 across a river from Dai Loc District Headquarters.

My principle task was dealing with Vietnamese civilian casualties, usually caught in the crossfire of night battles. During the day, I went out to see them or deal with other related matters at the various line company and combined action platoon positions in our tactical area of responsibility. The scattered line company units (located in rice paddy swamps or on jungle hilltops) were usually platoon sized, and the combined action platoons (located in and around hamlets, which they were assigned to protect) were effectively about half the size of a Marine infantry squad (that is, seven to nine men).

At night I returned to the command post, unless out on an ambush patrol. When under attack, which was almost always at night, Headquarters & Service Company Marines defended this hill, as well as running any patrols related to its security. The Marine Corps has never been long on its supply of infantrymen, so Marines not in the line companies had to do their part too. In the Vietnam War, any isolated firebase was a target of attack.

It's fairly clear that the incidents described in the vignettes can't be connected together as a single narrative of experience. They're snapshots, and the narrator of each one isn't the narrator of any of the others. These "snapshots" were written as focal points of discussion. I spent my first six and a half months in Vietnam with the infantry battalion and the final six and a half months of my tour at 1st Marine Division Headquarters Forward (operationally known as Task Force X-ray) at Phu Bai, a large combat base with an air strip eight miles south of Hue City. Here I was part of G2, intelligence. Any overview I may have obtained of the Vietnam War came from this latter assignment.

The Marines who assault the hamlet in this vignette have no doubt as to the stiff opposition they'll encounter. They know it to be a fortified hamlet. Nevertheless, there are civilians. This is war, and any war is anything but clean and simple. The Marines take casualties in this assault, and the Viet Cong are killed to a man. This isn't the way the insurgents would've preferred to have it, but the Marines were able to show up in force unexpectedly.

This long, protracted bloodletting in small battles, ambushes, mines, and sniper incidents was much the kind of war the 1st Marine Division fought in Vietnam. The 3rd Marine Division, being closer to the demilitarized zone, fought a relatively more conventional war. An exception for the 1st Marine Division was the battle of Hue City, fought immediately following the 1968 Tet Offensive and directed from 1st Marine Division Headquarters Forward at Phu Bai.

A war of attrition such as this is very difficult for men trained as assault troops. Push forward and seize the objective. That's what animates them. Seize something, for God's sake! But what's there to seize, and if seized, how long will it be held? A moral dilemma such as this turns assault troops into hornets. They want to fire on anything, assault anything. It takes a great deal of discipline within the ranks to maintain fire and tactical control. But that discipline is precisely what's required to create high quality assault troops in the first place.

It's this element of discipline in warfare that gives it so much of its dignity and its high reputation (when that's allowed) among noncombatants. A nonmilitary person is apt to think of combatants as simply facing horrors. That's certainly true. But when those horrors are confronted under a necessary constraint, due to the complexity of the situation, the true magnitude of the character of good troops can be appreciated. When such character is exhibited, and exhibited consistently, the value of military training is brought into relief.

The American novelist and short story writer, Ernest Hemingway, once said that war was life speeded up. That's certainly the case here. In everyday life we face difficult situations that demand restraint combined with a determination to see them through. It would be simpler to blast in and immediately effect change. But few things work out that way. That's why the well-trained combatant is deserving of respect. What he does under the greatest stress and most frustrating circumstances, we do as well, but with a subdued sense of urgency. If the circumstances are similar, the stakes are not the same.

Unlike the civilian, the combatant never works for himself alone. He endures rigorous trials in close association with others and for others. There's consolation in this, in his not being alone and having the support of others, but there's no guarantee that his companions will survive to be with him to the end. What he must trust in is that they'll be with him for as long as they're physically able, and what he must give is the same devotion.

That devotion is the essential philosophy of life, any life. It's the core of what it is for human beings, communal creatures that we are, to live in this difficult world. It gives our lives meaning, but, though much desired, it's rarely achieved in civilian life at a level comparable to the military.

What Is War?

Combat Deaths

It wasn't much of a firebase: a platoon of Marines and some howitzers. Ours were 155 millimeter guns but the Army had a 175 there. If you were standing next to it when it was fired, the blast would knock you back a few feet. It could make for an unpleasant surprise if you weren't used to it.

The hill was an awful place. It was bad because we didn't have clear fields of fire. I don't mean we didn't cut most of the brush on its slopes. We did. But it grew back fast and the whole valley was jungle. That's why we were there: to observe VC traffic in the jungle. There was plenty of it but you couldn't see much. So we ran patrols in the area but they seemed to always know we were there. That probably had to do with the fact that there was a small hamlet nearby. The villagers there had a few miserable fields of things like rice and corn and they fished the river for shrimp with nets, but I don't really see how they got their living.

It didn't make sense. After we held that hill through several hard firefights at night and took heavy casualties, they moved us away and abandoned it anyway. We were even overrun on one of those nights, but that's not when they moved us. It was a few weeks later.

But the time I'm thinking of now was the morning after the night we were overrun. It was on one of our visits to the village. We didn't make many of them.

The choppers had come in the morning at first light to take out our wounded. But we still had our dead. Nobody had come yet from battalion headquarters with a truck to remove them. So we had the eight men killed in action, their bodies stacked like cordwood on the landing zone under army blankets with just their boots sticking out. A *couple had been killed by mortars, including one Army gun crewman. Most of the other dead were from the part of our perimeter where the Viet Cong had broken through the wire. They had hit one of our bunkers with a rocket-propelled grenade.*

John was my buddy. He had gone out with the reaction patrol, which tried to flank the VC assault with some diverting fire. I think it did help to break them up and that cut off the support for the ones who had gotten inside our perimeter. But John took a round in the face. That's what Sgt. Jeffers told me but I didn't want to see it.

I was sick of that hill. So was everyone else. So was John, long before he got it. Whenever the sun comes up you always feel good. It's warm and you can see. There's always a sense of relief. You got through the night. But that only makes you feel guilty when a friend has just been killed.

We had to go into the village the morning after we were overrun because—well, I'm not sure why we went into the village. Some guys from battalion headquarters showed up in a jeep with an interpreter and they needed a patrol for security. So four of us went along. There were three of them: a lieutenant and two enlisted, one of whom could speak Vietnamese. A little girl led us and we were very careful going down, keeping low and observing the brush. We let her get way out ahead of us. You couldn't see much and we didn't trust her. We didn't trust anybody in that hamlet.

She went out of sight around some brush and then there was an explosion. When we got to her she was lying there whimpering. There was blood on the grass and her left foot was gone about six inches above the ankle. You could see the splintered end of the shinbone, the torn muscle and blood pooling. I put a tourniquet on her. Then we carried her back up the hill and got battalion headquarters on the radio. That's where our company commander was. He sent us a chopper, which came from Division at Da Nang. It came over, barely touched down while I shoved the seven or eight year old girl into the arms of a crewman hanging out the door, then it went up again and became a dot in the blue sky.

What Is War?

We went back to the hamlet and the guys from battalion took care of their business, which now included telling the little girl's mother and an aunt, I think, that she was being flown to the civilian hospital in Da Nang. Then we climbed back up to the firebase.

What I keep remembering is that the little girl didn't scream or cry. She whimpered a bit; that was all. And we had been afraid to even trust her.

* * *

Death for us isn't an abstraction. It isn't so much an end to life in general as it is an end to *this* life:

I was sick of that hill. So was everyone else. So was John, long before he got it. Whenever the sun comes up you always feel good. It's warm and you can see. There's always a sense of relief. You got through the night. But that only makes you feel guilty when a friend has just been killed.

To say that it's warm and you can see is not just to say that you're alive. It's to say that you're alive in the world. Sensations of sunshine, warmth, and fresh air are coming in through your senses. You're responsive and react to them with thought and feeling. So, being alive is very much a matter of being a part of this world, entering into its processes, modifying them, and being modified by them. Life is never only ourselves. It's everything that's a component of our daily awareness. This is what we can't bear to lose, either in ourselves or those we care about, when we say we fear death.

Grief in war is like any grief in life, with one exception: It seems to gather all the various modes of loss into one instant of emotional impact. Death in combat is usually young death, the extinguishment of a life that has all or most of its potential ahead of it. It's death in close association with other men, involving a mutual dependency of each upon the others, such as is found in the closeness of a family relationship. It's death by common enterprise. The man in your unit who dies in combat has by some inexplicable arrangement of fate drawn the unlucky number that could've just as likely been yours.

There's one other terrible reality. A feeling of guilt is enhanced in the survivors by the realization that they're glad it wasn't them. Each of them had hoped it wouldn't be him, and now that very hope looks like the mechanism that brought about the event. In short, it's good to be alive, and it wasn't a good thing for the one who died that he did so. How is it possible for this to be fair?

War introduces death and serious injury, not as an occasional unpleasantness, but as the chief protagonist in the drama. It's the business of combatants to kill other combatants and to mistrust any persons who might turn out to be in league with the enemy. That was the situation with the little girl in this vignette. The local farmers had seemed to have been aiding in the concealment, movement, and resupply of the enemy. When the girl stepped on the mine, her misfortune made it clear that she, at least, was innocently unaware of any enemy designs.

So what's the unique character of these things? It's the bold relief that human life is placed in. Life as imagination, wonder, feeling, comradeship, innocence, and design—life, as everything that makes it what it is, is made crystal clear to the human mind in war. Few people know life in all its worth as the combatant does, even though he's in the business of taking it. That's why so many veterans return home changed as they do—some to live disturbed lives, others to live much gentler lives than they'd ever considered living before.

In civilian life, where death, injury, and sickness are generally spread out over a greater time period, it's possible, in prosperous societies at least, to evade the issue and ignore the inevitable consequences of living. In such comfort we're not as easily, especially for as prolonged a time, forced to face the central issue of living, which is that we're destined to die. But every day the combatant wakes up to this reality and hopes to safely sleep on it again.

What Is War?

So what's living? What's this thing so clearly seen in war, and the contemplation of which is so often avoided in peace? We know that living is thinking, feeling, being aware. But aware of what? After birth, the most important thing of which we increasingly become aware is that life is limitation. Not just some limitation, but limitation to the point of death and annihilation. Yet consciousness, the means by which we are aware of these things, is not limited.

Our conscious mind (not the content of it) is experienced by each of us as something indivisible and unlimited. It has no outer boundaries and can't be made into more than one consciousness. This is the opposite of what we experience in our bodies and the world around us. So a tension between these two facts, these two ways of experiencing ourselves and our lives, is immediately set up. We wonder: Which is the more true, the more dependable reality?

I can know that the content of my consciousness comes and goes. Many things jostle together and pass on through my mind. All these things are examples of limitation. For example, I can imagine two apples, taking up separate, limited areas of space. Then I can picture one or both of them being eaten, pulverized, or in some other way removed from its place. Or I can choose to stop thinking about them altogether. Something else will then occupy my mental space. So, everything that passes through my mind, including all my emotions, feelings, memories and perceptions, is an example of what comes and goes. It's an object lesson in limitation.

But again one thing isn't—the mind itself, that which we call consciousness. It's the clear bowl that contains all these other things. The sides of this bowl can't be seen; they can't even be imagined. Neither is it possible to divide one's own consciousness into more than one consciousness. Individual consciousness is both unlimited and indivisible.

Our certain awareness—or maybe we should call it an indemonstrable and unprovable intuition—our unprovable but compelling intuition of the indestructibility of our inner spiritual or mental being, our experience of this inner being as something unlimited and indivisible, is brought into sharp contrast with the obvious perishability of our limited physical person. The contrast is unacceptable. Our will finds the indestructible, or at least seemingly indestructible, core of our being to be the innermost, essential part of what we are. The will clings to this and says it should take precedence over any other fact about ourselves, yet every lesson of life is that we're physical and all physical things perish.

We never come to terms with this, and the normal human reaction, where possible, is to ignore it, to bury any thought of death, any fear of the cessation of our essential being—to bury it in things like religion and continual rounds of unreflective activity. When death suddenly visits, we're momentarily unsettled, often severely so, but we strive as soon as possible to return to our formerly unreflective state of mind.

War says no to this. It says, Here it is, come to terms with it. Here's death. Here's what life comes to. Every day and every night spent in combat, the possibility of losing his life, or of a comrade doing so, is the central issue set before the combatant. He can't ignore it. He may never resolve the issue of life and death. No one has. Religion leaves the question open as an issue of faith. It doesn't resolve it. And no philosopher has yet effectively done so to the satisfaction of those who've attempted to follow his speculations. But, in the name of all that troubles us, we wish he had!

Nevertheless, a combatant's awareness of the problem is heightened to a point that changes him and makes him knowing in a way that few others are knowing. He sees life as something stripped of illusion and, no matter how many years come to fade his memory, this knowledge of what he once saw, and cannot help but continue to see, is seared into him like a brand.

What Is War?

The Rhythms of Conflict

There are two kinds of rain in central Vietnam in the area around Da Nang and Hue. The first is the monsoon. It comes in a sudden downpour and disappears just as quickly. Overall at such times it's still the dry season. Everything is sunshine, heat, and white dust, dust that swirls so thickly on the roads you can only see the vehicle you are following if you are a few yards from it. But then the sky suddenly darkens and hammers down water by the bucket load. This only lasts about fifteen minutes, cutting deep gullies on any uneven ground. After that the sky clears and the world is sunshine, water sparkling on the ground and dripping. The green fields and jungle look as if they'd just been washed, and the local peasant farmers pay little attention to such rain, going on with their work as soon as it abates.

The second kind of rain is different. The sky is always cloud covered and gray, the temperature drops from the high nineties to the low seventies and the rain drizzles in an endless cutting spray. It goes on for months. The once dusty roads become sucking mud traps. Thick red mud. I once saw an amtrac, an amphibious tracked vehicle which is, after all, the size of a tank, with its whole bulk completely sunk into this mud. It was upside down with a big hole in the bottom. It had obviously hit a mine. Our vehicles couldn't get around much in this season, so we were dependent on helicopters for just about everything: ammunition, evacuating wounded, sometimes even for food.

But the mail. Now that was critical, and we only lost out on that once, in a third kind of rain which I haven't mentioned.

It was a flood. Vietnam is practically nothing but rivers. The jungle grows out of them like moss on a stream bank. The rice fields catch them and there is always more. Brown, sluggish and not too healthy looking, they roll about over the countryside like lazy sun bathing crocodiles. Until the arrival of a typhoon.

One night a typhoon hit our firebase. I don't think the winds got over seventy miles an hour because they didn't tear our hooches down. They just slapped the canvas sides around and made us wet, miserable and cold. When it was over we slept like dead men. We didn't figure the Viet Cong would be around. In the morning there weren't any rivers. Our hill was sticking up out of a lake.

By afternoon we had some of the villagers up on the hill with us. Not many. Most of them didn't trust us and preferred to stay down in the valley where the water was neck deep. The few villagers who joined us were sick. We put them in a hooch and covered them with blankets to keep them warm. A corpsman attended them and a guard was posted outside. There was a young boy with malaria, an old man dying of tuberculosis and a few others.

No mail. A wooden bridge from a few miles upriver was on its way down to take out ours, which was already submerged under fast flowing water, but that was all. There wasn't any mail because the choppers had to bring us our food and ammunition, all of it.

The next day the water was down to waist level, and after that it began to clear off of some of the higher parts of the road. This meant some of the old men could stand on dry ground and cast their nets for shrimp.

Now here was a people hit by war and floods, and they rarely had enough to eat. So what is their response? They go fishing. They laugh and joke. The children often play with undetonated mortars they find that then go off, and the young women step on mines. There is weeping in the family, but life, laughter, moments of pleasure, street market haggling in the village center, still go on. These people work in their fields while we or the VC shell them accidentally when trying to get at each other, and that accounts for the hunger, since crops are hard to grow in a battlefield. But they keep on working. We shoot up their villages, shell and bomb them when we think there are Viet Cong

What Is War?

in them. The VC too sometimes burn the hamlets and select uncooperative individuals to cut off their thumbs or assassinate them at night or even in the middle of the day. But they keep on going. What else can they do?

In Vietnam I have heard a kind of laughter which is clear and ringing like good crystal. I have never heard it anywhere else.

* * *

The rhythms of war have to do with many things that aren't always a simple matter of men and munitions. Not every conflict has been won or lost by bravery and ordinance alone. Simple endurance plays a role, and so do factors outside of a man's control. Weather and tactical reverses can repeatedly test the mettle of a military force.

One thing that must be employed is cunning. An enemy can be less disciplined, and he can be overmatched by superior force in the hardware of killing, but there's no guarantee he can be outmaneuvered on the battlefield. So, never knowing what to expect, men on both sides must learn to think quickly with as much mastery of the situation as can be attained under limiting, fast moving conditions, so they're able to change tactics on the killing ground, while operating under fire. That's why a leadership capacity that extends down to the lowest ranks is important. Where another man can immediately take over the command of a unit and continue to push forward toward its objective when the leader has been hit, the unit remains effectively in action and in support of other units.

Finally, disease takes its toll, so that the outcome of a military campaign may be altered by the ravages of nature. Here, good habits of hygiene are critical to success in the field. This is another form of discipline, no less important than command and obedience.

Of course, endurance is indispensable. Because of this, military men and women go through rigorous physical training to increase their endurance. Most importantly, they must become psychologically lean and supple, like the hard muscles of their bodies. Courage, which is an expression of endurance, is a complex emotion. We think of it as simply the ability to risk hazards. But it's more than this.

First, it must be distinguished from false courage—that which we're accustomed to call bravado. Bravado is the public display of risk taking, when there's a calculated sense that the odds are in one's favor. It's not bravery at all, but a sort of premeditated recklessness or appearance of it. It's useless for military purposes.

War isn't a game; it's not a show for public consumption. Along with childbearing, it's the most serious business to which a human being is likely to attend, and, also like childbearing, it's accompanied by blood, screams, life threatening risk, and the simple raw energy of living and propagating one's own peculiar pattern of life, if one can. War is about preserving or extending a culture, sometimes at the expense of another.

Bravery is certainly important; bravery does in earnest what bravado does in show. Bravery is courage pushed beyond ordinary levels by personal determination (that is, character), esprit de corps, and comradeship. It's what medals are given for, and in civilian life it has its mirror image in those who go beyond popular opinion to stand up for what they believe, since to brave personal condemnation and social censure is its own kind of hell. Most great individual achievements in both war and peace come from acts of bravery. But, like other military virtues, this trait is spread much more thinly through civilian ranks. That's why we first think of bravery in terms of warfare.

In general, Aristotle would define courage as the mean, or middle state, between two extremes. One extreme is insufficiency, the other, excess. In this particular case, the extremes would be cowardice and foolhardiness. Courage is the ability to hold to one's course under hostile circumstances, to neither lose one's heart (cowardice) nor one's head (foolhardiness). Courage can be induced and developed in young men and women through tough military training that emphasizes personal discipline and a strong sense of responsibility to others.

What Is War?

The most obvious characteristic of courage is endurance. Hard physical and mental training establish habits of endurance that not only prepare a combatant to undergo extreme physical and mental conditions; they promote quick and supple physical movements under fire and a capacity to make sudden, tactically sound decisions on the battlefield.

Though bravery is rooted in courage, it's the excess—the compounding of that virtue. So it's primarily courage itself in its universal form that sustains an army. Courage, both mental and physical, both in war and peace, is the soil the plant of enterprise flourishes in. When an individual has it, he or she is able to maneuver steadily through the obstructions of war, or the obstacles of life. When a nation possesses it, it's a strong nation. When held and trimmed to perfection as a core value in a military organization, here one finds a formidable opponent.

In the popular imagination, military endurance (the foundation of courage) becomes an example for all other forms of personal and organizational stamina. That's because, where the military is concerned, this virtue takes precedence over other considerations, causing it to become more visibly prominent than it would otherwise be. A military organization, when true to its warlike character and function, is professionally committed to a confrontation with life and death extremes. It wouldn't represent itself as being otherwise. Because of this, it becomes a perfect citadel or beacon for showing forth the characteristic of endurance and a consequent development of courage in the young men and women of its ranks.

War is, when closely considered, a characteristic condition of the entire world, and the world offers no apology for it, while it continually makes war on us. We develop and apply pesticides to destroy the armies of insects that attack our crops and homes. We use antibiotics to kill the little fellows we can't see who would harm us. We even go after those portions of our own bodies that would act out of harmony with the rest, applying surgical knives and numbing drugs to the offensive parts. In short, everything is in continual struggle and clash of arms with everything else. Only the armament changes in each case and, of course, the face of the enemy.

Weather is one of our most formidable opponents. It comes in the night, so to speak, since its mysteries aren't fully understood, and attacks us in our beds. It attacks individuals, societies, and armies alike, and it teaches us that adversity is in the very pattern of things. Someday, if we should completely master the weather, earthquakes, and other natural disasters, as we have many diseases, we may yet face on our horizon an asteroid the size of Rhode Island.

So why do so many people condemn war? Why do they do this, if the whole universe is essentially at odds with itself? No doubt because of its awesome destructive power (especially in modern times) and an uncomfortable sense that it's unseemly for a species to kill its own members. There's something against nature in this. But it's wise to remember that nature is often observed to pit its own forces against itself. There're no moral rules for the universe, other than the fact that every single thing is locked in a struggle with every other thing. Species replace one another. Individuals in a species drop out of the food supply to make room for others and insure the survival of the species. Planets die and suns burn out.

Those who'd rid us of war and military might say nothing of related factors found in their daily experience, such as police forces established on a similar principle of violence to protect their property and their lives. Neither do they remind us of the fact that they bolt themselves into their houses every night, attesting to the warlike nature of their fellow human beings. Would they get rid of police protection? Would they throw out laws and the enforcement of punishments? It would appear they wouldn't, yet they seem to think that if we outlaw international conflict, it'll simply go away. A United Nations with teeth, they contend, could rid us of the unending nightmare of war.

But I wonder if the dark corners of the human heart, unchanged by the international prohibition of conflict, might not go on finding other ways to continue the struggle against so-called harmony and peace.

What Is War?

Isn't this how terrorism works? Unfortunately, when examined closely, we see that peace in the human heart responds to different conditions than peace in the world. The internal condition can't be readily fixed by the outer one.

In fact, we might also take into consideration a legitimate desire to force change where lesser means have proven themselves ineffective. The American Revolution comes to mind. Even today, might not a stout and honest heart, if it were true to its nature, want to take on and defeat all those mundane social factors that presently encourage flaccidness of body, weakness of spirit, and that devastating boredom which inevitably goes along with the perpetual, droning condition of buying, selling, and mindless entertainment we call modern civilization?

So, if we really want to rid ourselves of war, we must look much deeper into the roots of our civilization for some of its fundamental material and spiritual causes. We Americans have an economy that demands a disproportionate and unfair (as seen by others) proportion of the world's resources. To get and maintain these things against the protest of outsider nations requires a powerful military. That's why our military strength is what it is. It's a tool for better marketing, more effective getting and selling across the globe.

Another thing we Americans should attempt to closely observe is the profound sterility and emptiness of our consumer culture. We have everything but what fills the human heart with joy and a sense of its own dignity. We have everything but the satisfaction of overcoming insuperable odds. Perhaps that's how we differ from the Vietnamese peasant living his precarious existence in the middle of a battlefield. He knows what he's made of. Many of us don't.

Human beings have a natural desire to discover and acknowledge their own measure against the measure of existence. It's a basic need. And those of us who acknowledge this need would also like to develop an ability to recognize where it's legitimate and not legitimate for us to contend with the obstructions of life. How far should the human will extend? How much should it suffer suppression?

That's to say, we want to discover these things if we're honest and pure in self-examination. We want to because we know that if we don't take an uncompromising look into ourselves, an aching for such truth will remain somewhere deep within us. As a result, young men and women will continue to find ways to seek it out. They'll likely be drawn into the military because that need in each of us demands it of them, that need to continually renew their knowledge of what their proper place is in the general scheme of things.

The military and war teach this knowledge with an uncompromising truth. It's the uncompromising nature of the military experience that appeals to them. It's not something they can hear described. It must be experienced to be understood.

The protagonist in Ernest Hemingway's short novel, *The Old Man and the Sea,* having reached his own accommodation with life, puts it this way:

> …it is good that we do not have to try to kill the sun or the moon or the stars. It is enough to live on the sea and kill our true brothers [the fish].

In other words, it's enough to find our proper place in the world and know the difference between a possible and impossible enterprise, between a fitting and a ridiculous struggle with the conditions of our existence.

Guerrilla Versus Counterinsurgent Operations

The first time I saw her was not a pretty memory. She was the bride-to-be taking part in a traditional Vietnamese wedding procession. It was a beautiful day and you could smell the green rice wafting in from the fields. She was dressed up in a white ao dai, the classic long slit dress with matching long silk pants, which always looks good on the women, especially when they're young. And she was.

We were guarding a bridge just outside the village. It was a temporary pontoon bridge which had only recently replaced a permanent steel one that had been blown up by the Viet Cong. There was a lot of bad feeling at the time because some of the guys believed that sympathizers in the village had been responsible for what the VC had done. There were five of us on the bridge and the same number of Marines had been killed there before.

So when the procession tried to cross, we refused to let them. That started an argument. The groom got excited—it was his party—and that only made things worse. Cpl. Thomas, who was in charge of the rest of us, was a big guy with dark bushy eyebrows, a square face that gave the appearance of an iron jaw, and a beard shadow that was plainly visible after he shaved.

"That's it, buddy," he said. He grabbed the groom by the shirt and pulled him up to his face. "You're not going across, and if I get any more crap from you, you're going in the river."

That's when the little priest in his black cowl stepped up. "Take your hand off him," he said.

Tollefson

Cpl. Thomas released him. "Look, Father," he said. "Nobody's coming across. You understand? Khong duoc lai day."

The priest said something to the groom and they all turned around and went back to the village.

Well, the story was bigger than the facts. I'm not saying we should have behaved the way we did. But that damned priest laid it on thick to the District Chief. Then the District Chief went to the colonel in command of our battalion, since he was responsible for security in Dai Loc District, which was part of the battalion's Tactical Area of Responsibility.

The Colonel had two of us in front of him, the Corporal and me, since I was second in charge of the bridge detail. The canvas sides of the hooch were rolled up so that warm air and sunlight flooded in. The Colonel looked very neat and clean.

"Corporal, what is this I hear of you and your men beating up several members of this man's wedding party?" The groom was present in the hooch, which was the Colonel's office and which we were standing in side by side, rigidly at attention just inside the door.

"Sir, that man is not telling the truth."

"There were others present, and there is a priest who was also a witness."

"Sir, I don't like to call a priest a liar."

"Corporal, I don't give a damn what you like or what you think you did out there. Your job is to provide security. Now that bridge is on a major transportation route. People have to cross it. Your duty is to screen them, not beat up unarmed civilians."

"Yes, sir."

"Do you understand me, Lance Corporal?"

"Yes, sir."

"I'll court martial both of you, the whole damned lot of you, if I hear of anything like this again. Now get out of my sight and perform your mission like Marines."

"Aye aye, sir." We did an about-face and left.

Walking back to the bridge, Cpl. Thomas seemed to be mulling it over. Finally he said, "That little sack of..."

"Hey, man, we weren't exactly civil, you know."

"One Marine is worth twenty of them. You saw what they did to those guys. What makes you think they weren't just checking us out for their guerrilla buddies?"

"Maybe," I said. "I don't know."

Several weeks later and much to everybody's surprise, the VC mortared the village.

"Hell of a way to treat old friends," the Corporal remarked.

There were quite a few casualties. The Colonel sent an interpreter and a corpsman down to the bridge to give first aid to some of the wounded. A young woman approached, and I saw that she was the bride from the wedding party. She didn't look as young and pretty. Her face was drawn, her white cotton blouse was smudged with dirt and had some blood stains on it, though she wasn't wounded, and she burst into tears when she got to us.

The interpreter translated.

"The VC came and took my husband away. I don't know where they have taken him. They said he didn't pay the tax, but he always..." She stopped and looked at us with fright, especially at Corporal Thomas. He listened to the interpreter without saying anything.

The interpreter told her to go to the battalion command post. He accompanied her. From there she was sent to the District Chief. Eventually, through the grapevine of village informers, the local Vietnamese officials were able to find her husband's body. It was buried in a mass grave a couple kilometers from the village. The heads of all the corpses were missing and the bodies were bloated, stinking and starting to come apart. But she recognized her husband's somehow. The heads turned up later in another nearby pit.

* * *

To get a sense of what it's like for a civilian populace to live between two opposing forces, you have to witness it and observe with compassion. This compassion demands empathy, since the only way to form a sympathetic understanding of another person's plight is to attempt imaginatively to stand in his shoes. That can be difficult where trust doesn't exist.

A guerilla war generally places a civilian population in grave danger. These people not only live in fear of the insurgent forces operating in their area, they must find a way, if possible, to avoid reprisals from the opposing force which suffers casualties from the guerillas. This is especially true if the insurgents seem to be operating with impunity amongst the people in question.

Under these circumstances, of not knowing when to trust the population while conducting patrols and other operations among them and against opposing guerilla forces, restraint among the troops becomes a difficult task. It's only natural that the Marines here felt bitter resentment concerning the loss of their fellow Marines. Consider that the majority of combatants are usually young and inexperienced in life. They're also trained to be aggressive and make quick on-the-spot decisions. None of their soldierly experiences or functions are conducive to a calm and careful analysis of the humane dimensions of a situation.

Yet, in attempting to suppress an insurgency, that's what is required of them. They must, as it were, have eyes in the backs of their heads. They shouldn't only understand the tactical expediency of a situation. They're called upon as well to exercise long range foresight and corrective hindsight. This is because the ground they're fighting for isn't just a set of grid coordinates on a terrain map. It's the hearts and minds of a people.

An insurgency is meant to filter through a people, becoming immersed in them, then flow back out fortified with their allegiance. For this reason, guerilla forces operating in any area will work tirelessly to convert the people to their cause. They'll use persuasion where possible, but if some of the people resist, they're more than willing to bend them to their way of thinking with force. They can do this because they come from these people, speak their language, eat their food, and live and operate in their territory. They're also able to single out uncooperative individuals for selective assassination, providing an example to others while not immediately threatening them.

The conventional forces opposing the guerillas don't often have these advantages. Even if these forces are made up from the native population, they're generally gathered from all over the country and quartered or garrisoned in parts of the country they may never have been to before. As a rule, these conventional forces attempt to make up their disadvantage in access to the people with greater resources in long range mobility, supply, and coordination and sophistication of armament.

The success of this precarious balance of superior armament against greater local influence is always in question. If insurgents feel overwhelmed by greater force, they can dissolve into the countryside. They can conceal their arms and hide among the populace. In other words, they can disperse themselves throughout a number of hamlets and villages for the moment and regroup at another time or even in another place. But not so the conventional forces. It's this comparative difference in flexibility that makes insurgencies possible.

Now add to this the arrival of a foreign power, called in to assist in the suppression of the insurgency. First of all, they come because the home grown force is too weak to do the job alone. That in itself is an indication of the growing strength and success of the insurgency, not to mention the increasing support for that insurgency, willing or unwilling, that must exist among the people.

On top of this, these new forces don't speak the language, have never eaten with or lived among the people, and are generally unsympathetic to either them or their foreign, and therefore often incomprehensible, customs. So what's the immediate experience of these troops? Probably recent casualties from an enemy that isn't always willing to face them directly and which they consequently tend to view as being cowardly. This, in spite of a demonstrated fighting prowess when the insurgents actually are encountered.

There's also a tendency among these foreign troops to view the local people as not only being aware of what's going on in their midst but of being complicit with the enemy. "How else," one of these combatants might ask, "can these things take place before the people's eyes? Either they know about it or they don't. They clearly must know about it, and they do nothing to warn us. That means they're involved."

There's one other consideration. Troops sent to die anywhere are going to assume possession of the place where they might possibly "buy the farm." "It might not be our country, but we're paying for it." All these things can add up to a hostile, tense, and overbearing situation.

That's what appears to have happened in this vignette. The people may be trying to walk a thin line between two forms of annihilation. But the complexity of their psychological dilemma is rarely seen or understood by the two interested military forces. Expediency is the military rule of conduct. Survival is the civilian concern.

So the questions that must be asked are these: Whose country is it? Does it belong to the strongest party, or to those who live there? If it belongs to those who live there, does that imply that the guerillas have a moral advantage, since they come from at least some of the people? Or if it belongs to the strongest party, who is the strongest party? Only the victor will know. In the meantime, just how savage should the struggle become? It is, after all, a war. How should the people be treated, given the treachery of some, which are usually a hard to determine faction? What's permissible in terms of coercion of the local populace in order to find and close with the enemy?

All these questions are asked of the conventional forces, particularly the foreign troops. It's been assumed the insurgents have already chosen a path that, due to their determination to use and control the people, will become increasingly vicious and cruel toward those elements of the population who appear to refuse support.

What Is War?

The Moral Uncertainty of War

We could see them down on the road. Actually see them planting the mine about a quarter of a mile from us. Not far. It was Sunday afternoon. We were taking it easy sitting on the hooch steps. It didn't really matter that it was Sunday, only what day of the month it was. The day of the month determined the number of days you had left in Vietnam.

A jeep pulled up. The first sergeant from Mike company got out, then hauled out his prisoner. A patrol had picked him up for trying to peddle marijuana to some of the troops. The first sergeant grabbed the prisoner by the shirt. He had an ordinary shirt on, not a peasant's smock. The first sergeant yanked him out of the jeep, then, as he was stumbling forward, slammed him back against the side of the jeep. The prisoner's hands were tied behind him, so it was just a balancing act to see if he could find a way to stand on his legs.

"So you speak Vietnamese," the first sergeant said addressing himself to me.

"Yes."

"Well, tell this asshole if I catch him peddling junk to my men again, I'm going to cut off his balls. You hear that, asshole?" he said, turning back toward the prisoner and giving him another shove. "Goddamn VC!"

I figured the prisoner was in his late thirties, but it's hard to tell. These people are born old and die young. Meaning they're worldly wise. They always know what's going on and they seem to always look about the same age once they're grown. Until they get old anyway. They get old in their forties.

Tollefson

I've never been in the place where they put this guy. There's a hole in the middle of our helicopter landing zone, and they put him down there underground. The French built the cells down there as part of the fort on a hilltop overlooking a river that we used for 3rd Battalion headquarters. We had gotten orders from the 7th Marine Regiment that he would be picked up by helicopter when one was available and taken to Division headquarters. They must have thought this guy was into more than selling marijuana.

Before we took him to put him down that hole, the other guys were taken care of. The ones planting the mine in the road, two of them. A volley of three shells was fired. They had variable timing devices on them and their effect could easily be seen from our hilltop position.

They exploded in black puffs one right after another directly above the heads of the two Viet Cong. Thousands of needles rained down on the two figures. Of course, you couldn't see that part from a quarter mile distance. A patrol was sent out to see what we got.

The first sergeant had two other guys with him, a corporal and a lance corporal. They got out of the jeep and were the ones who took the prisoner to his holding cell. The first sergeant and I walked along behind them, while the first sergeant explained to me his hopes of starting up a boy scout troop among the local village kids.

The corporal was stocky with hairy arms. He held the prisoner with his left hand on the prisoner's left wrist behind the prisoner's back where his hands were tied together. With his right hand he had a hold on the shirt collar which he used to shove the prisoner forward. The black lance corporal held the prisoner in the same way on the right side. Twice on the way to the helicopter landing zone the corporal kicked the prisoner in the back of the legs. The second time the prisoner fell to his knees. The lance corporal cuffed him on the side of the head with the back of his hand and jerked him back to his feet.

The first sergeant paid no attention. He wondered if I'd mind doing a little interpreting for him in starting up the boy scout troop. I tried not to sound enthusiastic because the idea seemed ridiculous to me.

What Is War?

When we all got to the hole the prisoner had a tired look on his face but didn't say anything or show any resistance. They put him down there in the dark.

* * *

There's no way, whether in a high intensity war or low, to prevent the hardening of troops. It's a matter of survival and of seeing their comrades killed or severely wounded. The amazing thing is that they often return home to lead extraordinarily peaceful lives. So the question on moral grounds would be this: Given this flexibility and resilience of the human psyche, precisely what is the basis for our moral rules, and why must they be different in war?

Perhaps the flexibility and resilience we speak of here might be better termed adaptability. A different face for different worlds. But that would imply insincerity, and there's nothing more spontaneous and true than the pared down emotions of the combatant. The returned veteran, when able to make the necessary adjustment, isn't usually found to be lacking in sincerity either. Even those who remain disturbed over their unforgettable combat experiences are precisely those who aren't able to reconcile such different worlds, and they're fighting this emotional battle in the very depth of their souls.

I've mentioned before that the grounds for any moral system are essentially twofold: First, trust is the core, heart-centered condition underlying the establishment of moral relations. Second, there's the physical and economic setting that determines the specific nature of the laws and customs of a particular people.

To this latter might also be added the historical traditions of that people. These traditions might've been conditioned by their present physical and moral setting or they may've been carried over from other lands and circumstances, as in the recent colonization of the Americas by Europeans or the invasion of the Holy Land by ancient Israelites.

Physical and economic circumstances change from place to place, creating a varied set of mores and laws for each setting and society. As just mentioned, tradition, or historical inheritance of both a technological and moral nature, also plays a role, sometimes causing the moral character of a society (in terms of both its unity and outlook) to be at variance with its present physical and economic circumstances. This accounts for the sometimes slow technological, social, and military advance of a society. That society must iron out its major contradictions first.

A comparison of the United States and Mexico might help to make this clear. Because the people and culture of the United States has remained more uniformly what it was in the majority of people who immigrated to it during the period of its national development, there's been more room to adapt to new physical and economic circumstances.

In Mexico two quite distinct peoples came together. They produced a hybrid race that bears the marks of both cultures. Much of what lies between these two cultures has proven incompatible, and Mexico has spent nearly half a millennium working out the differences. As the people there become more homogeneous, this impediment to a more rapid national development will likely change.

War, as mentioned previously, inverts the role of the physical and economic and converts it to the sphere of amoral relations between contending states or military forces. Here the physical and economic character of the force in question is employed in whatever manner is most certain to destroy or defeat the opposing force.

But each military organization on either side retains trust as the principal bond between its own combatants fighting together against an opposing force. More importantly, it deepens the bond to an extraordinary level not seen in the more relaxed, laissez-faire civilian world. But this very deepening of the bond obstructs an empathetic approach to outsiders, especially if they're seen as in any way hostile or untrustworthy.

What Is War?

If we return to the questions asked at the end of the last chapter, we may obtain an understanding of the moral problem. First, there was the question, Whose country is it? Does the land being fought over belong to its indigenous inhabitants or to the strongest contending force on the ground? We see immediately that this isn't an easy question to answer.

We could apply a moral maxim, such as the right of an indigenous people to inhabit their ancestral land. But in the country described in these vignettes, that people was divided into what appeared to have been a civil conflict. Which side was right? Probably the Viet Cong and the North Vietnamese would've argued that Vietnam belonged to the Vietnamese, and that what was occurring was no civil war but the last and greatest of the colonial wars. The United States, seen in this light, was just another aggressive Western power with colonial ambitions in Asia, where it didn't belong.

Aside from its stated preoccupation with preventing the spread of Communism (which interference in the affairs of other nations worldwide was carried out on the dubious premise of a right to self-defense), the United States might've insisted it had been called upon to help a free and democratic nation preserve its liberty. (It did often publicly make this claim, as it has in other wars, large and small.) But freedom implies choice, and the choice of the Vietnamese people was never clear.

If the situation was unclear, how about the right of strength? Well, that really was the issue the war was fought over, as is ultimately the case in all wars. It turned out the American people lacked unity and resilience in this matter and withdrew their support from the enterprise and, unfortunately for the outcome, their troops as well. The Vietnamese Communists (or nationalists) did not, so they lost most of their battles and won the war.

But then, isn't that the nature of guerilla war—to employ one's own weakness in such a strategic manner as to defeat the stronger opponent? Their weakness was largely material, or economic. So they kept the combat initiative in their favor as much as possible, using hit and run tactics. The physical environment—a half mountainous nation largely covered by rivers and thick, junglelike growth—tended to work in their favor.

But their principal strength lay in their resilience and uncompromising determination. If there wasn't total unity in the South Vietnamese people, there was a determination on the part of those who were Communist to oppose Western aggression until the last Viet Cong or North Vietnamese soldier had died. Nationalism is a powerful incentive and shouldn't be lightly toyed with.

These points aside, we can now ask, How should the people have been treated? Again, the answer turns out to be thoroughly ambiguous. If we say they should've been treated humanely as noncombatants according to present civilized standards, we run into the dilemma of defining a noncombatant. Some of those guerillas were farmers by day, using the identity of noncombatant status as a cover for hostile actions. Then again, some, perhaps many, of the people were truly sympathetic to the Communist cause and, though noncombatant in status, were harboring and aiding the enemy.

(I refer to Communism advisedly here because I believe the insurgent movement in Vietnam was largely nationalist. The insurgents would probably have adopted any doctrine that would further their cause. Communism had the advantage of emphasizing the good of the society over that of the individual, which was a tenet already present in Far East Asian culture.)

But not all the people were sympathetic to the Communist or nationalist cause. My own impression as an interpreter going among them was that the majority of them in my battalion's area of operations were indifferent to the political outcome of the war. What they wanted was the right to go on living their lives in the manner to which they were accustomed. That turned out to be very difficult for them, so they aligned themselves with whoever could exercise force against them at the moment. This involved a lot of switching sides from day to day, week to week, and month to month. That, of course,

What Is War?

looked like duplicity, or treachery, to all the combatants and angered both military forces engaged on either side of the struggle.

So that brings us to a final, previously stated question: What's permissible in terms of coercion of the local populace in order to find and close with the enemy? You can't trust some of them, but some of them are truly innocent. That dilemma affected both sides in the conflict, and does so in any modern war where civilian populations are so inextricably mixed in the fighting. Even in World War II a significant portion of the civilian populations were working in war supporting occupations, manufacturing battleships, bombs, bullets, food, and other supplies for the troops in the field.

The entire civilian population of a nation can be employed, one way or another, in creating the infrastructure that vitally supports the war effort. Should these people be killed, as in the fire bombing of Cologne in Germany? If not, the war effort may be lost. If so, how many of these people had a real choice about what they were doing? Even if they chose to do it, how much information did they have to support an opposing view? In short, a good many of these people may've been technically innocent.

But "No matter," says the writer of these words callously. You can't get any kind of a clear grip on these distinctions, and once committed to war, it's all or nothing if you hope to win. In other words, war is a matter of expediency and, once engaged, the rules of civilized community are ipso facto (by the fact itself) denied and put aside. The only true moral community that remains, both in the field and at home, is the one in which all are locked together in a deadly struggle with the other side.

But this doesn't rule out individual acts of humanity by combatants, nor the careful consideration of any brutal use of force against an unarmed population. Great discipline and caution should be used wherever it's possible. But this'll never be enough to give warfare the name of a civilized or moral undertaking.

The Socialization of Combat

You could hear the explosion for miles around. It was a big mine and when the bus hit it, that was the end of the bus. It was a local bus loaded with Vietnamese peasants going from one district market center to another. The Viet Cong must've meant that mine for one of our tanks or thick-hulled amphibious vehicles because the bus was shredded up like tin foil. You couldn't even make out what it was.

We were running a patrol nearby and had a radio and a corpsman with us, so we went over to check out the damage. We approached carefully because road mines are often followed by ambushes. When we got into the rice field next to the dirt road where the remains of the bus were, we started finding bodies and parts of bodies. All over the place. It was sickening. There were pigs and chickens scattered around too and some of them were alive. Then we discovered that some of the people were alive as well. Maybe half a dozen.

We found a woman lying in a twisted position on her back next to a paddy dike made of packed earth with grass growing on top. She still had all her limbs intact and had only minor cuts, but she was unable to move and just lay there looking up at the blue sky. The corpsman knelt beside her. He felt her in different places and tried very gently to straighten her body and make her comfortable.

"I don't think her back is broken," he said, "but I think just about every other bone in her body is."

He felt along one of the black silken legs of the woman's peasant pajamas while she watched him with a kind of apprehensive trust. She was a young, good looking Vietnamese. Vietnamese women are almost all beautiful when they're young. Before the beetle nut they chew ruins them by turning their mouths red and their teeth black, and before their faces get pock-marked from poor diet and sickness. It's the slender build, but with a figure, the small boned features and the long shiny black hair that do it.

"See," he said. He pulled her pant leg up to the knee. There were several black and blue spots along her shin and at one place about half way up the skin was broken and you could see a jagged piece of white bone. She winced when he barely touched her leg with his fingers.

Sgt. Sanchez came over. We were shin deep in paddy water and the woman was also lying in the water, but with her head propped against the paddy dike. "I had Baker radio for a helicopter," he said. "We found a couple more over there. They're in pretty bad shape."

"Like this one," the corpsman said.

The sergeant stood there contemplating her for a moment, then turned around and walked away, sloshing water in his jungle boots and crushing bunches of healthy green young rice plants into the mud under the water as he went.

When the chopper arrived our corpsman was dressing the wound on a little boy about five years old. He was found sitting alone out in the same rice field. He was sitting up in the water whimpering, looking at his right hand which was almost completely severed at the wrist, hanging by a tendon or two and a piece of skin. I don't know what gave him the presence of mind at that age, but he was holding his wrist tightly with the other hand, cutting off most of the flow of blood. It saved his life. Even then there was enough blood in the water all around him to make it appear as if there couldn't be any left in him. This boy had been blown the furthest into the field of any of them. The few survivors must have been the ones riding on top of the bus with the chickens and pigs.

Just as the chopper touched down, pushing the water away in waves with its prop wash, there was a thud, then a couple more, and a patter of several more bullets hit the water beside the helicopter.

We all went down into the water.

Tollefson

"Sniper, damn it! Johnson, get a couple people and go around that tree line. See if you can get in behind him." Everyone was returning fire and it was pretty clear there was only one VC out there from the way the rounds came in, one at a time with three hits on the helicopter's landing gear and a few extra in the water.

I took two members of my fire team and we worked our way around to the left at a low run through the water. Hard going. He wasn't taking any more pot shots at us, but we didn't know if he'd taken off or was still lying in the tree line.

On the other side we caught sight of a young Vietnamese male, dressed like any other peasant, running as fast as he could along a dike away from us. All three of us fired almost simultaneously and he fell with a splash into the cold, early morning paddy water. Behind us the helicopter rose into the air, taking out the worst of the wounded Vietnamese.

* * *

I've discussed at length the problem of empathy in war. It might be worthwhile now to examine why it should be a problem for any human being. In other words, why is empathy important to human beings? What if none of us had any empathy? What if another person's pain never bothered any of us, let alone trying to imaginatively understand that pain on a personal level?

First, it should be pointed out that, while empathy is a product of imagination and therefore a characteristic most likely confined to those primates nearest us on the evolutionary ladder, sympathy extends further among other forms of life. Most dog lovers have seen it in their pets, and elephants are reported to return at times to elephant "burial grounds" and handle the bones of the deceased. Precisely how much imagination goes into the elephant and dog behavior, I don't know, but certainly sympathy, or some kind of emotional awareness, is evident.

Since we humans with our grief, burials, and religious hopes are clearly involved with one another at a sympathetic level, there can be no doubt that these emotions must be accounted for in any situation where human death and pain exist. We're social animals, as are elephants and dogs, and, therefore, as the English poet, John Donne, put it, "a part of the main."

We don't exist as isolated entities. We belong psychologically and emotionally to humankind. Our lives obtain their meaning from our interactions with other members of our species. A human being alone without others of his kind and without the capacity to even imagine other people, wouldn't be a human being.

So, given the fact that we possess the emotional capacity for sympathy, as well as the imagination for empathy, it stands to reason that we must either practice empathy or refuse to do so. Combatants, though highly empathetic towards members of their own unit, often refuse to exercise this emotional and imaginative mental state toward others. That's because it's hard to love those who're trying to kill you and for whom you're attempting to perform the same unsympathetic service.

But this very withholding is often put aside in the case of the apparently innocent, as is evident in the situation described in the preceding vignette. Here the Marine patrol takes some risk of ambush and snipers to come to the aid of wounded civilians. Even in this situation, these men have learned to view death and suffering with some degree of detachment, but not such detachment as would preclude a sympathetic, perhaps even empathetic, response.

For example, the narrator of this vignette is willing to acknowledge the beauty of Vietnamese women, as he gets close enough in imaginative sympathy to observe the complexity of the wounded woman's emotions, which he could only do with some empathetic involvement, albeit restrained. He, the Navy corpsman, and other members of the patrol extend sympathy to the boy and other wounded. Otherwise, why would they be there, taking a risk and interrupting their patrol?

So, we must first posit the fact that empathy is natural to human beings and tends to emerge wherever circumstances don't forbid it. Of course, war is one of those circumstances that do forbid it, but even in that case the control may be selective. Human beings may also be desensitized by a corruption of taste in the culture of which they're a part. That's increasingly evident in our American television, film, and hard music environment, where violence is often seen as not involving pain or suffering.

But, nevertheless, it's reasonable to assume that human beings naturally tend in varying degrees toward a warm, imaginative involvement in the pain and suffering of others, especially where they have some personal connection with those individuals. We've said this is because they're naturally social, feel emotions, and have a faculty of imaginative identification. All of which makes social life not only desirable and possible, but necessary.

How does this work? The social instinct is perhaps the hardest of these three elements to explain, as instincts are apt to be. Human instincts are particularly difficult because we live inside of them, so to speak, and can't easily see where a personal volition might not be entirely free. But let's look at the social instinct. I'm going to describe an experiment I once performed as a boy of eleven or twelve while living in the Philippines.

I, loving animals though not always kind to them, was in possession of a flock of chickens, among other things. In this flock was a young White Rock hen. I'd raised her from a chick. At the time in question, she'd just reached maturity and was laying. However, she had no sense of propriety about the business, and was in the habit of flying up onto our charcoal grill and letting loose with an egg, which fell in a clean, plumb line trajectory toward the carport pavement, where the grill was located. This annoying habit brought her to my attention.

What if it were possible, I thought, to turn her overnight into a mother? Would it work? I knew she'd just begun laying, had never deposited her eggs sensibly in a nest, and certainly had never been known to set a nest of fertile eggs or brood any chicks. In other words, she hadn't done all the things necessary to either become or be a mother, other than randomly dump her potential progeny on the concrete apron of the carport. This absence of any experience of the functions necessary to become a mother would seem to imply that the instinct of actually caring for chicks would not come independently into play.

I decided to find out if this were the case, so I went to a local Filipino barrio (hamlet) and bought a brood of newly hatched chicks right out from beneath the wings of the mother. I brought these home and shut them up in a small box barely large enough to contain them and the White Rock hen. In this way, the chicks were forced to remain under the hen's feathers, since there was no other place for them to go. The box did have a screen door on the front.

I don't remember, but I must've kept them that way for about a week. Surely I fed and watered them. I don't remember. At any rate, that's how they lived for a week, and there was only one mishap. On the first day, the hen pecked at one of the pesky chicks dwelling under her and blinded it in one eye.

This is how it turned out: After that week of enforced coziness, I released the hen and chicks into my backyard with everything else that inhabited it. From that moment forward, the hen treated the chicks as if they were her own. She clucked for them as they fed together in the grass, keeping any from straying too far, and she brooded them under her feathers at night. It seemed, I reasoned, that she'd simply "forgotten" they weren't her chicks, so she treated them as though they were.

What I'm alluding to here is my belief that the activation of an instinct isn't something hard-wired into an animal. A particular instinct doesn't necessarily fall into a definite sequence of behavioral patterns, each stage in the sequence being required to bring the next one into play. It's simply a tendency toward a pattern of behavior, which is easily evoked. In other words, the hen didn't need to go through the stages of laying, setting, and brooding, each stage following the previous one in a definite progression, to arrive at the business of caring for chicks.

In this case, the hen lived closely and long enough with the chicks to begin to experience them as a part of herself. Once this occurred, she took care of them as she would her own body. That's like a mother, human or otherwise, who'll sacrifice herself for her children. It also resembles the spontaneous behavior of a combatant who sacrifices himself for other members of his unit.

The development of the human social instinct begins in infancy. (By development I mean activation.) Our parents and siblings are an integral part of our environment and, as soon as we're able in any way to interact with them—especially to obtain things that please or displease us—they become, outside of our own bodies, the most fascinating part of our environment. They become in a certain sense a part of ourselves. Not entirely, of course. They don't always do what we want. But then neither do our bodies, our emotions, or our minds.

This fascination with and growing interest in others extends to more human beings as we age and our social horizons widen, and one of the most important things we learn is that we get along better with people if we have some concern for their welfare. But, most importantly, this increasing knowledge of our relationship to other human beings, which is learned by trial and error, is continually reinforced by the unconscious process of simple identification. Those who're most important in our lives are perceived as being somehow a part of us. We look after their interests as we would our own.

To the extent we don't feel threatened, we can extend this sympathy indiscriminately to other human beings. But, of course, we also learn that some people would obstruct or interfere in what is in our own best interest. So the exercise of the social instinct is always qualified.

Now empathy is a tool for better extending sympathy, so we learn the value of practicing it where we can. But where human beings are aligned against our interest, we must suspend empathy to prevent a confusion of our emotions and a scattering of our purpose. This

What Is War?

happens in society. We distinguish between friends and enemies, but hopefully not to the point of doing our enemies deliberate harm, except in self-defense. It would disrupt the social bond of trust in society as a whole if we attacked some of its members simply because they got in our way.

But, as we mentioned before, war is different in this respect. We owe no allegiance to those who would harm us or our society. We owe them only the enmity of a self-defense posture. In combat this is pretty cut and dried. The enemy is definitely going to kill us if we don't destroy him. However, what the combatant doesn't know is how the politicians of the opposing powers got into the posture of enmity in the first place. For myself, I know of few wars that haven't somehow begun over a series of trivial and dishonorable doings perpetrated by both sides of the impending conflict.

This, as I said, is not generally known to the combatants. The sacrifices of the combatants, made in the cruel and brutal crucible of war, ought to be seen as pure and honorable. But the politicians, and the national mood behind them, may yet be called to account. Often, in analysis, any war can be reduced to a simple matter of economics, national ambition, and a lack of empathy extended beyond the boundaries of the feuding nations.

War as a Reflection of Life

She was nine years old. The bullet went into her left cheek and came out her neck on the same side. It must not have hit anything solid like teeth or bone because the damage wasn't that bad, though it wasn't pretty to look at.

It was her sister's fault. She was carrying a rifle when we spotted the two of them crossing a rice field. We ordered them to stop but they didn't. So we fired, two or three guys in the patrol, and that brought them down. Killed the older and wounded the younger one. The rifle was an AK-47. Pretty sophisticated for a mere peasant.

Our corpsman patched up the little girl and we radioed for a chopper. It took fifteen minutes for the helicopter to get there. She'd probably have bled to death if the corpsman hadn't put compresses on her face and neck. Nothing major had been severed, but the wounds were bleeding quite a bit, especially the one in her neck.

After the chopper came we continued our patrol. Our platoon encampment was in a swampy area, partly stuck back in some trees beside a rice field. It was a miserable place. We had sandbags strung out in the wet places for stepping stones. What a mudhole!

The lieutenant wasn't with us when the thing happened but he took a special interest in the case. He kept wondering how she was doing, so one day about two weeks later we went in to see. She was at the civilian hospital in Da Nang. The lieutenant had some other business at 1st Marine Division Headquarters and that was our excuse. He took me along.

What a stench bucket of a place that hospital was. It was a complete joke. They didn't seem to have anything in the way of supplies. The morgue was in a separate building. It was a bare room with its door hanging ajar and containing a couple of bodies and a lot of flies.

When we entered the hospital a doctor met us in a small room at the end of a long hall. There were a few bottles of this and that and a few medical tools I didn't know the use of. For the most part the room was just empty and dirty.

When we entered the hall, the lieutenant, a short, young, kind of peach fuzz looking guy, stopped and stared. All along both walls were people sitting in silence. I mean absolute silence. They were all women just sitting there on the floor, some holding children. Several of the white cotton blouses were blood stained and, as we walked along, the three of us, I saw that one of the women was dead. Another, several really, had very small children in their arms. And one of these was holding a child that was also dead. I can't explain death, but it has a kind of presence. It's as if a personality had suddenly left the room. You always recognize it.

In this hall the silence alone was enough. Not even the children made any sound.

"This morning VC come in. They mortar the village. We don't know what was their reason. Maybe the people won't give them taxes. Maybe they are too friendly to Americans."

The lieutenant listened to the doctor and nodded. He also kept looking up and down the rows of people lining either side of the hall. We walked quietly between them.

Upstairs there was a room full of South Vietnamese Army soldiers. I just glanced through the door as we passed and saw that the beds were so close together you couldn't see the floor. There were a lot of people in there, and they were noisy.

This was a two story building, and since we were on the second floor it was as far as we could go. The hall was bare with a few windows lining it on one side, the recovery rooms on the other. The windows were dust streaked and only let the light in intermittently.

At the far end of the hall was a tiny room. In the room was a straw mat. No window. It was more like a closet than a room. Kneeling on *the mat was the girl we had shot. Her wounds looked almost healed and there were no bandages on them.*

The lieutenant knelt down and asked her in English who she was—what her name was.

The doctor translated for him.

"What village are you from?" And so forth. That's how we found out the woman we'd killed was her sister. As she told us, she cried quietly.

Afterwards, on the way back in the jeep, I kept looking over at the lieutenant. He sat on the passenger side looking out over the fields, his M-16 slung across both arms, pointing out towards the fields on the right. The normal procedure is to have the selector off safety for immediate use. But he left the rifle on safety. He left it that way all the way back to our little home in the swamp.

* * *

As we continue our philosophical investigation of war, we discover that our questions persist in centering around the specialized topic of ethics. That isn't surprising, since we're talking about life the way it's lived and asking ourselves how it is people normally behave, while comparing it to how we think they should behave. If war is, as Hemingway referred to it, "life speeded up," then an investigation of it may broaden one's understanding of life in general. This is because, according to Hemingway's view, you find everything in life you find in war. But war concentrates the experience, stripping it of civilization's habits of pretense and avoidance of reality. For this reason, the study of war from the inside (not the justification of it) is the study of life as it truly is.

It's a terrible subject. Stripped of all the layering of social ritual and the insulation of myth, life seen in its bare bones is brutal and terrifying. Few human beings can bear to look upon it for long. (This is the meaning of mortals being unable to look upon the face of God, who is a reflection of the truth we see in ourselves.) The veteran, of

What Is War?

course, must learn to deal with this reality, which is buried deep within his emotional core. He can never live quite as comfortably with the deceptions of civilization as others do.

What do I mean by these deceptions when I speak of them as social rituals and the insulation of myth? I'm not debunking religion, as might seem to be the case. Religion in the purity of a founder like Moses, Jesus Christ, Buddha, the Hindu scriptures, or the Tao Te Ching is not myth or insulating ritual. It's full of the wisdom of life. But religion never remains as it begins. Clear vision is a rare trait among human beings. Distortions set in almost as soon as a religious tradition is founded.

There're two reasons for this: One is that institutional religion is primarily about social control, not clear insight into the human condition, either spiritually or naturally. The other is that most people would rather not think about life's critical issues. It's difficult and painful. So what begins as radical insight ends as a comforter for the weak in mind and spirit.

The great founders of moral insight (here we would include Socrates and Confucius with Jesus and Buddha) appear on the scene prepared to sacrifice everything to accomplish their mission. They're not looking for comfort so much as truth. But their followers, the further away they live from them in the timeline of history, aren't of a similar temper. They're more interested in comfort than truth, even if it's at the price of self-delusion. Thus the change in perspective. And the beginning of myth, which is the conversion of moral insight into the insulating self-deception of comfort religion.

This momentary digression into topics far beyond the subject of war is meant to put it into perspective. The relationship I want to suggest is that the nature of war has an immediate bearing upon our understanding of the character of life. For that reason, we can make another digression into the broader field of general ethics.

In the preceding vignette the narrator and the lieutenant were clearly disturbed by the brutality of conflict. But the full meaning of this brutality hadn't come home to them until they saw it perpetrated by their enemy. The Viet Cong had deliberately shelled a village, killing innocent civilians. Why did they do it, and was it any different from shooting the girl and her sister?

For general purposes, let's propose a simple code of ethics. This will not only be applied to war but to life in general, since war in reality is inextricably blended with life. In constructing this code we should leave out any considerations that would apply to specific societies. We should deal only with what might be pertinent to them all.

Let's put down five principles. They are, first, to embrace *life* with all one's heart. Second, to practice *empathy* with all one's reason and sympathetic imagination. Third, to express *kindness* with the consideration of a sound awareness as to how, to whom, and in what circumstances it's applied (where legitimate self-defense doesn't prevent it). Fourth, to act out of *sincerity* in every matter of mind, body and soul. And fifth, to be *thoughtful* (concerning one's own motives and the motives and circumstances of others).

Life, empathy, kindness (with a caveat), sincerity, and thoughtfulness. This doesn't look like it has much to do with war, and it does seem to have a lot to do with comfortable living. But what I want to point out is that it comes close to describing the core precepts of all the great religions. That doesn't make it a replacement for them, nor does it suggest they can all be reduced to just these principles and therefore blended into one super religion. It's simply a stripped down approach to a purely ethical outlook, and it's based on the view that the great religions at their core are founded upon fundamental insights into the human condition.

To say that we should embrace life with all our heart is to say we should be honest about it. We should look at life without any blinking of the eyes. We should have a positive attitude about it. By positive I mean that in thinking about life we're thinking about ourselves. We are life. We're life in its bare bones, with all its pleasures and joys, with all its imaginations, and with all its brutal shocks and disappointments.

What Is War?

To limit ourselves to our minds and emotions or even to our bodies is a falsehood. We're every other person and thing. We're the whole of all that is our experience, our decisions, the decisions of others, and the full complexity and range of consequences. We're the wildflower upon the hill under an open sky, and we're the bleating fawn crushed in the coils of a python. We're the python too.

This isn't an idealism, a splendid vision, a work of the imagination. It's fact. When we make divisions and choose what pertains to ourselves and what doesn't, this is originally done for reasons of practical necessity. We must get our living, often taking it from the mouths of others. The flaw comes in when we apply it theoretically or imaginatively to our true nature—that is, to life as we actually experience it, whole and complete. That's why the Native American asks forgiveness of the animal he kills. He knows he kills his brother.

To say that we should practice empathy with all our reason and sympathetic imagination, is to insist that we recognize the underlying truth of this oneness of all things. We know that the suffering man, the terrified fawn in the coils of the snake, the fearful cow slaughtered for its meat, are all parts of one whole of joyful, hopeful, suffering life. Man's range of hopefulness is only greater, by the aid of reason and imagination, not different. We should be able to see this and to put ourselves into each of these conditions of life, and we should be willing to do so because that's the way life is.

To say that we should express kindness with the consideration of a sound awareness as to how, to whom, and in what circumstances it's applied (where legitimate self-defense doesn't prevent it) is to reiterate what an empathetic understanding demonstrates. Empathy teaches us how to feel all conditions of life. To feel them, especially their pain, is to will the amelioration of pain.

The practical way of doing this is to practice kindness intelligently. I say intelligently because misapplied kindness is no kindness at all. We must understand where and when it'll be truly effective and where and when not. For instance, to allow a criminal to go repeatedly unpunished isn't a kindness.

"Where legitimate self-defense doesn't prevent it" is a deliberate caveat. This isn't a moral precept. It's a practical consideration which stands outside the moral sphere. It must often be employed and is consistently employed where expediency has replaced moral concern, such as in a state of war, or in the punishment of a criminal.

The warring party and the criminal have set themselves outside the moral sphere, except, in the latter case, where the proper and proportionate application of laws is concerned. Any time an act truly demands self-defensive measures in response, both the act and the self-defense are ipso facto amoral. For this reason, war is always outside of morality and can never be justified according to any moral precept. So is the punishment of a criminal insofar as the *execution* of the punishment is concerned.

To say that we should act out of sincerity in every matter of mind, body and soul is to refer back to the first principle I've listed, which is that we should take an honest and open-hearted approach to life. If we act out of sincerity in all that we think, do, and feel, we put ourselves in an honest relationship with ourselves and our lives. We don't allow ourselves to be fooled by ourselves or by others, and we try our best to keep others from being fooled by us.

This is, of course, hard to do in everyday life. If we revealed all the facts about ourselves to others, they might, and probably often would, use the truth against us. But any variance from the rule of honesty in dealing with others is a matter of expediency—self-defense—and therefore outside the moral sphere. Even in the case of expediency, though it may be necessary to control the facts of a matter in self-defense, it's never necessary to represent one's state of mind or emotions to another in a false light.

I am, of course, referring only to matters of personal bearing. I'm speaking of sincerity, not a revelation of plans, strategy, etc. Remembering that all people are a part of the unified whole that is life, we can find the means for treating them with the respect of an honest *expression* of whatever business it is we have with them, even if that business is in its nature unpleasant.

Finally, to be thoughtful (concerning one's own motives and the motives and circumstances of others) is, first, to pay attention to oneself, to examine oneself. Socrates said, "the unexamined life is not worth living." In describing the Noble Eightfold Path, the Buddha spoke of such things as right speech and right conduct. In other words, are our thoughts and words uncharitable, do they deviate from the truth, and what are the motives behind them? What are the motives that prompt our actions? Know thyself, Socrates insisted. Jesus asked, "What good will it be for a man if he gains the whole world, yet forfeits his soul?"

To know who we are is the basis of being who we are. Then to correctly understand the motives and circumstances of others (insofar as this is possible) is to know the rest of ourselves, since we're a part of the main, or the whole of humanity and ultimately all things. When we act with more certain knowledge and do so with sincerity, we're more likely to behave justly because we're acting in accordance with the true nature of things. An act is generally considered fair, or just, when it's in harmony with the facts.

This simple code of ethics, stated in five principles, is the briefest, most succinct expression of a moral outlook on life I can come up with. So, how does it apply to warfare? In two ways: Within the structure of a military unit these rules all apply. Outside that structure they don't. Why not? Because war, however it originates, is a matter of expediency, of throwing off the consideration of any moral outlook. Either side in the conflict, whether acting as an aggressor or not, is in a position of self-defense. That's the expedient condition that overrules moral behavior.

Two military powers at war, whether they had a choice in the matter or not, have been placed in a position of moral anarchy. Any rules of conduct they come up with for governing their interaction, such as the treatment of prisoners, are simply matters of expediency. I will treat your prisoners humanely because I want you to treat mine the same way. Such rules are almost always disregarded because the foundation of trust that makes morality possible is already broken.

The Right of Military Interference

They hit Larry in the stomach. The bullet went into his side and there was a lot of bleeding. We were crossing between two rice fields on a dike, going carefully, watching for trip wires, when that first shot was fired. It struck Larry and we all went down in the warm water and mud ooze to form a defensive perimeter around him. After that you could see the bullets hit the water in front and to one side of us and you could hear the faint whistle when they were close overhead. We waited for mortars, searching the tree line for movement.

"Get a compress on him! Stop this bleeding!"

The corpsman crawled up and John, our squad leader, moved aside to give him room. He rolled onto his back, his rifle in his hand above the sloppy water. There was a leech on his bare forearm and he brushed it off leaving a tiny trickle of blood.

"They're over there to the right," he said, looking over his shoulder at the tree line. "We need more cover. O'Connor, Johnson, Delaney, over on the right!" he shouted.

The three whose names he'd called started directing bursts of automatic and semi-automatic fire toward the right side of the tree line. The rest of us got up, myself and another guy supporting Larry under each arm, and scrambled for the patch of brush jungle that was only about fifty feet behind us. Larry was getting weak, unsteady on his legs, and weighed a ton, it felt like. He wasn't a big guy but we were trying to run in muck and water.

When we got into the brush, which was so thick you could hardly crawl into it, we spread out in a line and started firing at the Viet Cong. You couldn't see much, even in broad daylight, but we had a

What Is War?

clear idea of where they were now. Our base of fire let O'Connor, Johnson and Delaney get back to us. Larry was still our only casualty.

"Mathews," John shouted, "get a round in there. Damn it, what's taking so long?"

I could see Lance Corporal Mathews fooling with his grenade launcher but I don't know what the problem was. He got two rounds off and the second one seemed to do the job. The shooting stopped, except for a couple shots fired from our side.

When the last shot was fired, John scrambled over to have a look at Larry. I was lying beside Larry, one hand on the compress bandage, trying to slow the bleeding. Larry was almost unconscious.

"Hey, what are you doing?"

The guy who'd helped me haul Larry into the brush had his canteen out. I guess he'd been planning to give him some water.

John knocked it out of his hand as he came up and shouted. "Idiot!"

John and Larry were good friends. Larry was my fire team leader, the first fire team. He would take over the squad if something happened to John, that is if he hadn't been wounded himself.

Larry was real woozy. He smiled at John and just kind of rolled his eyes and grimaced. We didn't have a radio.

"The lieutenant should have heard us," John said.

"We going over there?" I meant after the VC to see what we'd done to them, if anything.

"No, we got Larry to worry about. Take McDonald and find O'Connor and go get the lieutenant. Tell him we need a chopper."

When the three of us got out of the brush we saw a patrol approaching us about a hundred and fifty yards out and realized it was with the lieutenant. McDonald and O'Connor went to tell them about the medevac and I went back to John, Larry and the other guys. Larry was out, white as a sheet.

"Is he breathing?" I asked, almost in a whisper.

"Barely." The corpsman was attending him, doing what I'd been doing with the compress. He'd given him morphine but Larry hadn't *really made an issue of the pain. John was sitting a little ways off, his knees drawn up, his rifle in his lap and his face in his hands. When I went over to him, he said, "We'd better check it out."*

On the way over to the other tree line, we heard the helicopter. It came down in the middle of the rice paddy. The two guys we'd left behind with Larry ran out to the chopper and then ran back to the brush with another guy and a stretcher. Because they went for the stretcher and didn't just bring Larry out, we knew he was dead.

* * *

In a conventional war, the fighting is concentrated, like a sheet of rain in a monsoon. But in unconventional warfare, the fighting tends to be sporadic, sudden and unexpected. It doesn't generally involve the clash of large scale units. Of course, this depends on the circumstances. Even in Vietnam the war was different for the 1st and 3rd Marine Divisions. The 3rd Division, being deployed next to the demilitarized zone, fought larger scale engagements against North Vietnamese Army units. The 1st Division fought a hit and run war against smaller, hard core, supposedly southern, guerilla units. Though these guerilla units were called Viet Cong, by the middle of 1967 both divisions were mostly engaged in fighting against North Vietnamese Army regular soldiers (even when designated as Viet Cong), and both divisions seemed to suffer the same casualty rate overall.

The different kinds of fighting were determined largely by access. In the north, up against the demilitarized zone, North Vietnamese Army units could easily move in and out of the area of conflict. They'd infiltrated further south as well and did sometimes fight there as fully integrated North Vietnamese Army units. But they also replaced the original southern members of the hard core Viet Cong units, since the southern fighters had been largely exterminated by that time.

What Is War?

The nature of modern guerilla warfare, as described by the Latin American revolutionary, Ernesto "Che" Guevara, in his manual on guerilla strategy and tactics, is reflected in the way the Vietnam War progressed. Briefly, his theory advocates three phases of insurgent operations. In the first and earliest phase, when the insurgents are relatively few in number and weak, they should concentrate on hit and run tactics by small units or even operate independently as individuals who pose as citizens by day and fight by night.

In the second phase, as guerilla numbers grow and their weapons improve, the guerilla style of hit and run tactics remains. But now the units are larger, "hard core," full-time units operating from sanctuaries. The third phase is conventional. It takes place after the enemy has been demoralized by continual attrition of its numbers in casualties and by unsuccessful results in its attempts to stem the insurgency.

All these phases took place during and immediately after American participation in the Vietnam conflict. In the northernmost provinces, where the Marines were, and elsewhere in South Vietnam as well, the first two phases were mixed together, with an increasing movement toward the second phase. The third phase occurred after the American pullout of ground troops, proving once again Niccolò Machiavelli's assertion in his short treatise, *The Prince,* that if outside troops are brought in to aid local combatants, it's a clear indication of the latter's weakness.

This raises the question, Why were American forces introduced into the conflict? As in most wars, little matters grew into big ones. We financially supported the French effort to recolonize Vietnam after the end of the Second World War. After the French left and the South Vietnamese government proved both unpopular and unstable, the United States began to introduce military advisors to help them counter a growing insurgency rooted in an opposition to the original French involvement. Helicopters and air support followed. Finally, we sent ground forces, and the number of American troops in Vietnam reached a high of over half a million by 1968.

On a psychological level, the United States ignored the fact that the war was nationalist in character and that the South Vietnamese government was unpopular. The problems in government led to problems in military leadership of South Vietnam's armed forces. This resulted in a demoralization and lowered combat effectiveness of South Vietnamese troops. America's direct entry into the war with ground forces was the final blow. It said the South Vietnamese couldn't do the job of defending their own republic.

The problem for philosophy is, What constitutes a legitimate right of interference of one country in another country's affairs? Given the fact that such interference is often incremental, as it was in Vietnam, was it at any time justified? Stopping the spread of Communism was the major excuse offered for America's military involvement. This would shift the emphasis to America's confrontation with Soviet power.

War isn't always a state of conflict. It can simmer under terms of peace for years, as was the case with the Cold War. Looking closely, we see that America and Russia at this time represented opposing political and economic philosophies. The goals were political, but the underlying drive was economic. American Capitalism needed a wide range of markets and supply of resources in the world, and the expansion of Soviet influence threatened to significantly reduce these. The United States resisted this threat by attempting to stem the spread of Communism to other countries.

These issues, political and economic, were debated and carried out in terms of expediency. Remembering that there's little genuine trust between nations, as, on the contrary, there should be between individuals within a society, it isn't hard to understand the self-defensive posture of nations toward one another. The posture implies the complete abrogation of moral principles.

In a cohesive society there's an attempt to establish and maintain justice. Within that society, justice may be defined in various ways. It isn't necessarily democratic or directly representative. But it must be based on some generally accepted system of relations between people and classes of people that establishes social harmony. Without an atmosphere and practice of mutual trust, social cooperation would be impossible.

Between nations this doesn't apply, even between allies. This is because relations based on trust must involve a willingness to make concessions to support the atmosphere of trust. People in a relationship based on trust agree not to do certain things considered mutually harmful to one another, such as murder, calumny, and the destruction or dispossession of property.

But nations think only of their own interests. They enter into agreements with other nations to further those interests. They agree temporarily on what they think they have in common. These kinds of agreements, based entirely on self-interest and involving no real foundation for trust, inevitably lead to disagreement and continual shifting of allegiances.

Such a world isn't a moral one, because trust is the natural basis for a development of ethical rules of behavior. It involves a willingness to make long-term concessions in behavior and personal gain. In short, the international world of shifting, temporary allegiances to promote individual national gain is a state of anarchy, temporarily controlled in times of peace by mutual fear and selfish interest. It's a world governed by expediency.

On this basis, it can be seen that the involvement of the United States in Vietnam was amoral from beginning to end. However, it should also be noted that there's no possible moral basis for international relations, so long as we live in a world that sets national interest above other considerations. Even World War II, with its elimination of the horrors of Nazism and Fascism, was amoral. There's no such thing as a moral war. War is only about expedient solutions to practical nationalistic or ego-centered problems.

Thus, whether or not the United States should've been militarily or economically involved in Vietnamese affairs isn't something to be decided on a moral basis. It has no ethical ground. However, it can be judged on grounds of practical necessity, and, within that practical necessity, the issue of the killing and destruction caused by war can be raised. In other words, what's always at issue is, Will the suffering of the people of one nation, if war isn't enjoined, outweigh the suffering perpetrated both upon itself and another people, if it is?

Beyond this practical weighing of alternatives, any moral resolution of the problem of international relations would require a surrender of national interests and influence for the sake of establishing a genuine world community. But even this could prove unsuccessful, if human energies at the personal level weren't redirected toward more fulfilling goals than are offered by habits of individual arrogance, material consumerism, and the emptiness offered to lives lived as essentially isolated entities in isolated social groupings, or nations, both acting largely in their own interest.

The Social Responsibility of Warring Nations

They shot him because there was an order out to the surrounding villages not to swim in the river. We didn't want anyone trying to cross the river near our firebase because we'd just been through a North Vietnamese Army night assault. It was an NVA regiment designated R144. If we hadn't used the gunships, they'd have probably overrun us. So we wounded a seventeen year old from the village whom we later judged to be innocent.

We brought him up onto the hill to patch up the bullet wound in his shoulder. One of our bridge guards had shot him while he, as he put it, "was just going for a morning swim."

That's the way it was. You put out the word and they did stupid things anyway. They might as well go strolling in a mine field. But that was a privilege they always reserved for us.

The night attack came at two in the morning. That's usually when things like that would happen. It gave them time to get themselves and their gear up close enough to do something and time enough to clear out before dawn.

They slipped into the village across the river and set up their mortars. Then they started the barrage, walking the mortars in bright flashes over our compound and trying to hit the ammunition dump that they knew was in the middle of it. The mortars made a crumping sound like big hand grenades. As we woke up, dove into the mud puddles inside the low-walled sandbag bunkers beside our hooches, pulled on our pants and boots, and then headed with rifles and helmets (some with flack jackets) toward the perimeter, they crossed the bridge.

There was a bunker on their end of the wooden bridge and they hit that with a rocket-propelled grenade, killing all but one of the guards. The other one, who was on watch in about the middle of the bridge, they cut down with automatic fire as they went across.

By this time we were all pretty much in the trenches along the perimeter firing back. That didn't stop them. You could see them coming, intermittently. They were backlit by some flames on the smoldering wooden beams of the bunker. You'd see a shadowy figure or two in the dark and knew there were a lot more of them pouring over the bridge.

We sent a reaction platoon out to meet them. They lost a guy before they ever got to the bottom of the hill. Our eighty-one millimeter mortar crew finally got some flares up. The flares hung like balls of fire swinging from parachutes in the black sky.

We could now see the North Vietnamese soldiers hurriedly massing at the bottom of our hill. Some of them had on those helmets that looked like World War I helmets. When they started coming up the hill, they came in a line, shooting steadily, and we were getting heavy fire from the village across the river as well. It was hard to do anything but keep your head down. There was a smell of damp earth, brass and gunpowder with orders being shouted. I heard someone call for a corpsman way down the line on my right. Some of the NVA soldiers were using tracer bullets, so even if you were deaf and couldn't hear the rounds thudding into the sandbags in front of you, you could see how close the ones were that went over your head. You just waited for what seemed like a lull and jumped up, holding your rifle over your head firing a burst, and got down again.

Mike Barnes was right next to me.

"Did you see them, Corporal?" he asked. "They're coming thick as tent caterpillars."

A little ways down the line to our left, a Marine threw a grenade but it fell short and exploded without effect.

What Is War?

"It's hard to make anything out," I said. "The damned swinging flares are making shadows move everywhere. I can't tell if there're a million or a few hundred of them."

"I hope it's only a few hundred. God, I hope it's only..."

Then the choppers went up. The three helicopters lifted off our landing zone and circled around until they were directly over the massed NVA. One of them turned on its spotlight and the other two canted over to one side and went around and around it firing their M-60 machine guns out their side doors into the NVA line of assault. The tracer bullets came down out of those gunships in two pencil thin red lines. When they hit anything solid on the ground, they ricocheted away softly into the night like fireflies.

The assault was broken up and that made it easier to return fire, though we were still catching it from the village across the river.

Private First Class Barnes stood up, getting his head above the line of sandbags. He carefully squeezed a round off at one of the muzzle flashes we could see across the river. At the same time, with my rifle set on automatic, I emptied a magazine into the troops now broken up and running down the side of our hill near the bottom. As I pulled out another magazine of twenty rounds and shoved it into my M-16, I heard the most sickening sound, a kind of wet slap. Barnes fell down in the trench at my feet. His face was turned toward the ground but I could see the piece missing from the back of his skull, on the left side near his neck. The collar on his flack jacket was already soaked in what looked in the dark like black blood.

I was back in the States before I discovered I'd been wounded too. It was a pinhead sized piece of shrapnel in the muscle on my chest just below the skin, which I must've gotten while running across the compound toward the perimeter during the mortar barrage. I never even felt it, and it was the only contribution I ever made to that war.

* * *

Tollefson

Night assaults were de rigueur in Vietnam, when I was there. The rule was, Strike at two in the morning and that'll get you out and safely across the river before down. The river wasn't the one at the bottom of our hill. It was another river further off, that marked the limits of our tactical area of responsibility and the beginning of enemy controlled territory.

I've mentioned before that these vignettes aren't autobiography, and the narrator differs from vignette to vignette. What are portrayed in these vignettes are recombinations of things I experienced directly and things I didn't experience directly but have a good knowledge of. For instance, in two of the vignettes up to this point an M-48 tank plays a significant role. While in Vietnam I was familiar with these tanks because they operated in our area, but I was never inside one. However, in the late 70s I spent time in Boise, Idaho, as a tanker in a Marine reserve unit which was a tank company.

The night assault described in the previous vignette did occur on the night of November 7–8, 1967, but, though Marines were killed that night, none were killed right next to me as described. That's how these things were written. I'll give a few other examples for illustration.

In the vignette about the little girl shot through the neck, everything took place just as described, including the mortared villagers. With one exception—I wasn't in a line company. It was my job to go out to the line companies in my duties as a battalion civil affairs interpreter, so I'd been out to one of our platoon's bivouacs, which was in a swampy area near some rice paddies.

Again, the wedding procession incident was a matter I knew about from our investigations, but I wasn't on the scene when it happened. What occurred, however, had been described to me in detail.

The night attack on a hill in thick brush jungle in which a platoon was overrun did occur as described. It happened to one of Mike Company's platoons. I think it was the first platoon. But I wasn't a member of that platoon. I was the interpreter that arrived the next morning. We did go cautiously down to the hostile hamlet near the bottom of the hill, escorted by four infantrymen, and that Army 175 millimeter howitzer did throw me back against our jeep. But I wasn't on the hill during the assault the night before, though, of course, I knew about it as described.

The wounded little girl was fiction, but fiction only in the sense that the incident didn't occur in that time and place. We found other kinds of injured in the hamlet. It was these we'd gone to see—a hut full of people with shrapnel in the soles of their feet. One of the 60 millimeter mortar crew's rounds had fallen short the night before and had landed in front of their hut door. They'd all been sleeping on wooden beds with their feet facing that door.

I knew a lot about Vietnamese wounded. It was my job. War isn't clean, involving only combatants, and in a guerilla war especially civilians are frequently caught in the crossfire. I mention these things to give some sense of how the vignettes were written. This is important because no one could've played all those roles at once. I've mentioned this before. The vignettes are designed to provide a cross-section of the war in that time and place.

I was no hero, but I was a good Marine and did my job. I'm proud of that fact. I also can't forget what I experienced, because I saw death and suffering on both sides. Marines and civilians. Oddly enough, I never once saw a dead enemy soldier close up. The Communist guerillas and North Vietnamese regulars both worked hard to remove their dead so we wouldn't find them. So I saw them firing at us and us firing at them, but never saw the results on their side.

In one of the vignettes I mention a dead sapper on our perimeter wire. I knew about it. He was found lying there on the morning of the November 7-8 night assault. But I didn't bother to take a look at it because there were dead Marines to think about.

The questions the present vignette brings up are those concerning fear and death. Psychologically, we know what these things are, and militarily we know that the fear of personal injury or death and the horror at seeing comrades killed must be controlled. Men in combat do their best at this because they must. Unfortunately, it's later when they're home safe that they must unload the burden of this trauma. If they're discouraged from doing it by a hostile public, as happened during and after the Vietnam War, then they're forced to attempt to bury the memories.

Of course, that doesn't work. It creates emotional turmoil and sickness. From what I've personally seen and experienced of this, I'd say that the principal moral obligation of any people or persons is to receive their troops home as a part of themselves. If the war is judged to have been a mistake, it's not those who went to it who're most responsible for that mistake. They shouldn't be burdened with alienation or ostracism. Give them a comfortable place to heal their emotional wounds, for those wounds are the most plentiful of all the wounds received and they occur in every war.

Abstractly, we might go on to ask, Why *do* we fear death? Why does it traumatize us? It seems so natural to have this fear, we hardly ever ask this question, but understanding it better helps us to understand the human condition. It tells us why so many in civilian life avoid thinking about the issue of death as much as possible and why combatants have so much to deal with concerning it. I think the unwillingness on the part of some to confront death and suffering as a fact of life is the principal reason others are left to struggle with it alone.

Death, of course, is elimination of the personal self. We may justly believe otherwise, but that's no more than a belief and we know it. The facts which we daily witness tell us that everything which comes into existence in this universe goes out of existence. Even stars perish. How can we be different? Why do we want to be?

Yet, because of the indivisible and unlimited nature of our conscious being, we can't let go of the idea that that immaterial part of us is, or should be, exempt from annihilation. This makes us want to preserve the whole, to hold on to more than conscious being. We want to preserve the self, the personality, the will that is free to act and rejoice or suffer as a consequence of its acts. Hence the emotion of fear and the horror of death.

There seems to be only one moral solution to this problem insofar as it pertains to how we treat others in our social community, and it is that we should take responsibility for facing up to death as a fact both in relation to ourselves and to others. Whatever we may think of the fate of our souls, and however we choose to define it religiously or otherwise, we should first face the practical fact of our eventual physical annihilation, of the deaths of others, and of that tendency to make mistakes which is a universal characteristic of the human condition. Then we can go on to believe as we will, because that belief will no longer be an excuse for ignoring any truth about the human condition.

Reminding ourselves daily of the material limitations of life would insure that we're more compassionate toward others, because it would inform us that we're not only limited in living but in doing. We make mistakes. We should accept our own mistakes. If we do, we'll be better able to tolerate the misfortunes and failings of others. And we won't send young men and women to war, then turn against them for what we've had them do.

War as an international political act may be a matter of expediency and, as such, outside the sphere of moral consideration, but how we behave as individuals toward the members of our own community never is. For there in the community is the bond of trust that's the foundation of moral obligation. As we've freely taken up and benefited from this obligation one to another, we shouldn't abandon it when things become uncomfortable. I can think of no worse indictment of a society than that it should turn against its own.

Tollefson

Discipline as a Military Virtue

    Sam Houston really was his name. I don't think he was any relation to the first president of the Republic of Texas but you couldn't help making the association. He was a big guy with dark, curly hair. Kind of quiet, unless he was drunk.
    We didn't drink often then because beer usually wasn't available at our firebase. But they brought some in for us on Christmas Day so we could celebrate the twenty-four hour truce. Might as well relax while the Viet Cong had time to gather in their ammunition and rice.
    Sam was a forward observer. So when he wasn't out in the field with an infantry company calling in artillery missions, he did other things. Once they had him doing the daily burning of latrine receptacles. He loved that and did a lot of grumbling. Would even be sullen in the evening in the hooch with us. But normally he did more dignified chores when he was with us at the battalion command post. For some reason, the Colonel wouldn't allow him inside the Command Operation Center to do counter-mortar fire and things like that which would have been his normal mission. Though a good FO, he was considered too wild. So he went out early most mornings with the mine sweep team to clear Liberty road. The VC mined this dirt road almost every night without fail, and it was the mine sweep team's job to clear it of mines before the day's military traffic started passing over it.
    Here's what he told me one morning. We were casual friends and he wanted to talk, having just returned to the compound with the sweep team. It was about 8 or 9 a.m. and I was still lying on my cot, since I had the lazy job of a Vietnamese Interpreter.
    "Morning, Don," he said cheerfully.

What Is War?

"Forget something?" I asked. I had noticed the magazine, as usual, still loaded into his forty-five automatic pistol. He was also carrying an M-16.

"Oh yeah." He unloaded the pistol. "We lost our lieutenant today."

"The new guy?" I knew the lieutenant wasn't well liked. He was considered dangerous and naïve by the men who had to go out on these patrols with him. They provided security for the men who actually did the mine search.

"Yeah." He crouched down beside my cot, speaking quietly. "We were ambushed. The crazy, gung ho bastard took off after them over a rice field with his forty-five. Got shot through the head."

"Anybody else hurt?"

"No." Sam had the weirdest grin on his face.

On Christmas Day in the middle of the day a little U.S. Army one engine spotter plane flew over our hilltop position and dropped a box of books into our compound. I was surprised because I had always heard the Army was of the opinion that Marines couldn't read. On the same day one of our own trucks brought in a load of Red Cross care packages from 1st Marine Division Headquarters in Da Nang. They were full of odds and ends like gum, candy and a better quality toilet paper. That truck also brought the beer, enough for each of us to have two cans.

Not everyone drank. I didn't. And Sam got the extra beers. He got good and drunk.

In a way you couldn't blame him. For months the constant gunfire all around and the artillery and bombs in the mountains never stopped. Suddenly it was dead silent. It was unnerving.

Several of us were sitting in our hooch enjoying a big can of Spam for which we'd traded some Marine Corps combat knives to the Air Force in Da Nang. Christmas dinner, a few letters from home, and a card game. In comes Sam, waving his loaded pistol.

Tollefson

"Fuck this Marine Corps! Fuck you bastards! Screw Vietnam and all those damn VC getting their stuff together so they can come out and kill us tomorrow!"

"Take it easy, Sam."

"Put that gun away."

"Crazy fool. Don't you know you can't carry a loaded weapon in the compound."

He went over and collapsed on a cot, sobbing. Somebody quietly took the pistol out of his hand and unloaded it. A warm breeze flapped the canvas sides of the hooch. The naked light bulb flickered on its wire. We went back to our card game while Sam slept off the beer.

Later that night when we were all sacked out, except for the guard, the mortar crew decided to help out in the celebration. They set off a tear gas grenade behind our hooch.

The stuff was thick when it entered the hooch in the pitch black night. And when we woke up with burning noses, lungs, throats and eyes, we knew what it was. One guy fell vomiting on the ground as we ran along in our underwear toward the perimeter of the compound and fresh air, mucus pouring out of our noses. Two of us grabbed him up by the arms and kept on going through the dense fog of tear gas that followed us in a cloud.

Later when we came back to the hooch, we found Sam still dead asleep.

"Can you believe that?"

"Must be his mosquito net protected him."

It was worth a good laugh.

The next morning I told Sam about the tear gas and then asked him what had gotten into him with the beer and waving the gun around.

"I kept thinking about that lieutenant," he said.

It had been more than two months and I'd forgotten him. But it was only then that I realized what had happened to that lieutenant might not have been the result of an ambush.

* * *

What Is War?

From the perspective of military discipline, to frag (kill) a military officer is the most disturbing act I can think of. Personally, I don't positively know of any such thing having occurred among Marines in Vietnam. But there were rumors of such things, rumors that touched Army and Marine ground combatants in that war, and the incident described in the vignette is based on something I was told in the manner related in the vignette. That was as far as it got. I never found out if it was true.

It does bring up an important issue. The Marine Corps is known for its rigorous discipline, and the consistent high performance of Marines on the battlefield is a testament to its effectiveness. But, if it were true that such things as fraggings occurred among Marines or any other troops, a question must arise as to the nature of that discipline.

No one, I think, can argue with the basic military dictum that, "the difference between a mob and a military organization is discipline." This calls to mind such concepts as "fire discipline," "unit integrity," "working as a team, not as a bunch of individuals," etc. I don't know how many times as a young Marine I heard these things repeated in boot camp and at infantry training regiment.

They were critical to the Corps, as critical as a strong emphasis on hygiene, the buddy system, the fact of the noncommissioned officer being considered the "backbone of the Corps," as important as a reverence for military decorum, and the fact that the individual infantry rifleman is what the Corps considers itself to be built around.

Since the general topic of this book is philosophy of war, I will use the U.S. Marine Corps' stock of core beliefs as a means for discussing essential military values. The fragging of an officer, which implies a breakdown in discipline, is a clear violation of these values. So, how can we account for the possibility of such an act in a body of well disciplined troops? We'll begin our attempt to answer this question by putting such discipline and such values into their proper military context.

Tollefson

Esprit de corps is built into young Marines by a form of training that remolds them from self-centered, physically and mentally undisciplined individuals into men and women whose sense of self is to be a Marine. So strong does this identification of the individual with his or her Corps become, that Marines often go into combat fearing more that they may perform poorly as Marines than that they may be killed. They're taught Marine Corps history; they learn to respond to orders, to wear their uniforms with dignity, to take pride in a crisp salute and other forms of military decorum. These are all things that instill discipline and enhance their esprit.

Caesar, in his famous book, *The Conquest of Gaul,* describing his campaign in what's now France and the Low Countries more than two thousand years ago, mentions that the most important military virtues are leadership and discipline.

Poor leadership can result in a waste of first-rate troops. They can be led into tactically, or even strategically, compromising situations—as in falling into an ambush or fighting from disadvantaged ground, in the first case, or pursuing politically unclear goals and fighting under restricted rules, such as in the Vietnam war in the second case.

As for discipline, Caesar relates how the Roman troops conducted themselves in their campaign against the Gauls. The main body of troops was generally deployed in the now famous Roman modified phalanx formation. In the front lines of this formation, made up of maneuverable tactical units called cohorts, were the large interlocking shields of the legionaries. Each legionary was also armed with a short sword, which he could use to stab enemy troops as they fell upon him.

Clearly, keeping the shields interlocked and not breaking the formation under impact of the initial assault was essential. The need for great discipline is obvious here. If a man fell, the man in the rank behind him must immediately replace him. If a line broke, individual soldiers could be surrounded and cut off. The line must not break.

In one battle Caesar described, the Gauls rushed upon the Romans with wild, terrifying cries. They were big, long haired, rugged looking men. As they came on, their women ran before them, tearing their bodices and screaming that they (the Gauls) must not lose, for these, the lovely, exposed bosoms, were what they were going to lose, since the Romans would no doubt enslave the women. When these ferocious troops hit the Roman line with all the force they could muster, the line held. Having lost their momentum, the Gauls milled. The Romans moved forward and cut them individually to pieces.

Something similar occurred with the 1st Marine Division during the battle of the Chosin Reservoir in Korea. Surrounded by seven Chinese Communist Divisions, the Marines carried out an eighty mile fighting retreat to the port of Hung Nam. On numerous occasions, human wave assaults on the Marine lines took place during the night. At times some of these Chinese troops would break through a thin point in the lines. Once behind the lines, the Chinese would mill about, not knowing what to do to exploit their advantage. The better organized Marines simply turned around and destroyed them.

Again, the amphibious assault on the Tarawa atoll in late 1943 by the 2nd Marine Division ran into unexpected problems from low tides. Marine landing craft hung up on reefs offshore, and the troops had to wade ashore under extremely heavy fire from the Japanese defenders of the island. By the time these men got ashore, nearly every unit had suffered such casualties that the unit was tactically unable to perform its mission. Under brutal fire on the beach, these men reformed into fighting-capable units and pushed forward to take the island in three days.

These examples are mentioned for the purpose of emphasizing the role of discipline in achieving combat success. An effective military unit is carefully organized into a close-meshed fighting machine. It isn't a mob. That close-meshed structure, forged in discipline and held together by esprit, is what's called unit integrity. The members of that unit work as a team, not as individuals.

But unit integrity isn't limited to small tactical units, such as squads and platoons. Every Marine, Roman legionary, or well-disciplined soldier has an embedded sense of his larger strategic mission, however little he may be familiar with the details of it. He knows he must do his job because more than a few others depend on him. Many of the troops who form his larger unit of allegiance may be people he doesn't personally know.

During the occupation immediately following the 2003 invasion of Iraq, a squad of Marines ran up against a large, angry, Shiite mob, which was in an agitated and aggressive mood. The Marines stood on line, side by side, their loaded weapons extended before them. As the mob advanced on them, the Marines were ordered to move back one step at a time without losing their position in the line. They did this, eyes centered on the hostile mob, but without firing their weapons. The anger of the mob eventually dissipated. This is fire discipline.

So is sticking to your appropriate sector of fire in a firefight. These sectors of fire provide interlocking coverage of the battlefield. Without this controlled saturation of the enemy avenues of approach, enemy troops could easily find gaps in the opposing fire to exploit in getting closer to the lines and possibly overrunning them. This is fire discipline.

In Vietnam in 1966 a Marine reconnaissance team was surrounded and pinned down on a hilltop until it ran out of ammunition. The Marines continued their fight with rocks. This is discipline expressed with esprit.

Esprit de corps is further enhanced by an emphasis on such things as personal hygiene and overall unit hygiene when a unit is deployed in the field. There're practical reasons for these sanitary measures, but they provide a sense of caring as well. The buddy system also emphasizes the individual's participation with others. Rarely should a soldier or Marine be put into a foxhole by himself.

This is the military and its traditions, primarily described in terms of the U.S. Marine Corps, which reflects my background. These traditions are based on the simple virtues of mutual trust and cooperation, the central values of any cohesive social group. But they're more intensively developed within a military unit, a small community which is called upon at intervals to deal day and night with life and death issues.

What Is War?

Within that tightly knit sphere of trust can be found, in varying degrees, the more specific virtues of an unblinking sense of realism (that is, an embrace of life-as-it-is) and an empathy, kindness, sincerity, and thoughtfulness of its members toward one another. Outside the sphere of trust, there's only war and expedience. For without trust there's nothing.

Against this tradition of loyalty and mutual support must now be weighed the ugly possibility of a fragging, the deliberate killing of an officer, a member of one's own unit. In the vignette, the officer is a young lieutenant, described as naïve by the men who make up the security patrol under his command. He's also referred to as a crazy, gung ho bastard. In other words, he's seen by his men as being willing to sacrifice their lives for the sake of his own career ambitions or visions of personal glory.

This attitude on the part of the lieutenant is a clear violation of the bond of trust that should exist between himself and his men. The breach of that trust has dissolved the bond in the eyes of his men. Acting out of what they see as a necessary expedience in their own self-defense, they do away with him.

In expressing this point of view, I don't by any means affirm or condone what these men did. I'm simply pointing out that, where a bond of trust is established, it must be faithfully adhered to by all the participants in that bond. It was the lieutenant's duty to carry out his orders and his mission, even when at the risk of his or his men's lives. The men understood and accepted this. But when his interest turned in upon himself and away from a concentration upon an efficient execution of the mission, he set himself outside the bond. He set himself in the no man's land of expedience, and it cost him his life.

A parallel exists in the civil community. Here a criminal, who turns against his neighbors and unlawfully threatens their wellbeing, is punished. The right of punishment exercised by that society is based upon the assumed prior mutual agreement that none who participate in the bond of trust shall violate it.

Tollefson

Where the men in this patrol went wrong was in independently acting against their larger sphere of trust, their allegiance to the Marine Corps (and to the laws of the civil community they left behind). The lieutenant should've been reported to higher authority. But that's not always easy to do. The swift pace of what might be called the unending combat emergency decided the outcome.

What Is War?

The Fabrication of Wars

The first night of the 1968 Tet Offensive took out one of our Combined Action Platoons. The Marine contingent was made up of nine men. All we knew was that in the morning they were gone. No bodies. Nothing. As far as I know no one ever knew what became of them. The Viet Cong took their ammunition; their new, expensive night vision scope; the machine gun (they had a fifty caliber); even their C rations.

The Popular Forces soldiers that were with them also disappeared, though one of them later turned up in a nearby village. When we questioned him, he claimed the VC had thought he was dead and left him. But if that was the case, why were there no other bodies?

One thing we did learn from him, if his word can be trusted, is how they did it. They didn't attack the position and assault its wooden tower and sandbag bunkers. They just showed up after a previous action an hour or so earlier, suddenly appearing in the middle of the night in such numbers they overwhelmed the Marines and PFs.

How'd they get so close without being detected? I don't know. I know the Combined Action Platoon was short handed. They always are.

The battalion command post didn't sit quietly on its hilltop either. We were hit at the same time that the CAP unit was in that earlier firefight. The CAP unit was about a half mile away. I remember looking over in their direction once while helping to resupply ammunition to our own perimeter. It was easy to see that far from our hilltop, especially when the night was lit up with grenades and mortars. There were mortars coming in on us too and tracer bullets flying overhead but I still had time to notice the flashing lights of the explosions over there. As I was running toward the perimeter with a couple cases of M-16 rounds, I saw a long streak of tracers arc straight up into the night sky, followed by a shorter burst of fire. I wondered then who had gotten it. I knew those guys personally.

But as I said, I never found out. In their case, the night assault was just a diversion, a probing attack. It helped the Viet Cong figure out their defenses and numbers. An hour later in the dead quiet the VC just walked in and captured them.

Next morning we were busy with our own wounded and the choppers were coming in and taking them out. We had wounded from one of the line companies as well as from our own firebase. They were all on the helicopter landing zone. There was a volleyball net stretched across part of the LZ and plasma bottles were hanging on the net. Their clear fluid was carried down in plastic tubes to men who were lying close to the net.

"Arthur!" I said. He was one of my best friends but was over on the other side of the compound during the night with the heavy weapons platoon. I didn't know he'd been wounded. "What happened?"

"Took a couple rounds," he said. "One in the hip, one in the gut. Nothing serious."

Nothing serious? He was one of the guys with a plasma bottle attached to him. But that was Arthur. Glasses thick as coke bottles, a hooked beak for a nose, thick lips, pale blond kinky hair, and perpetual good humor. If he'd been dead he'd have had a comment on the funeral arrangements.

"Want to know what I think?" he said. I'd just handed him a lit cigarette and a chopper was taking off, blasting us with hot wind and choking dust from the prop wash.

"What?" I yelled, stooping over within two feet of him. The noise was deafening. He was smiling.

"I think they played their best hand last night."

"Who?"

"The gooks."

"Why?"

"Because it was organized. Too organized. You heard about CAP Charlie Two."

"Yeah."

"Must've taken a lot of planning putting that one together. Hitting us and them, then pulling back and walking in on them like that."

"I guess so."

"You guess so. Come on, man, when have you seen anything like that before? I've heard rumors..."

"Yes, I know. When S-3 called in our spot reports and casualties this morning, the Regiment told them Division Headquarters had said it happened all over Vietnam last night."

"Damn right. But we're after them now the sun's up. And we got a lot of air and fire power. They can't disperse as fast as they got together. We'll get them."

"I hope so."

He laughed and stumped his cigarette out on the ground. Two Marines came over and picked up the stretcher Arthur was lying on, one of them unfastening the plasma bottle from the net and laying it next to him. "So long, buddy!" he said. "See you back in La La Land." Just before they put him on the helicopter he propped himself up and looked back at me.

I must've been looking mournful.

"Cheer up," he shouted. "The war's over."

* * *

The term, La La Land, was an expression sometimes used to indicate Vietnam, and at other times it meant back home. Both places seemed equally unreal in those days, but in different ways. Vietnam was quite real in a gritty, fundamental, in-your-face sort of way. But it represented a kind of madness too, because war was never meant to be neat or trim. On the other hand, the country we'd left behind had become for us a distant, magical region of faded memories and imagined joys, from which unending and disturbing bits of news emanated, telling of protests, assassinations, and riots. These reports didn't resemble the calm, sane, antiseptic world we preferred to believe was our original home.

The Tet Offensive came unexpectedly to Americans on both sides of the Pacific Ocean. Though I think it was more of a shock "back home" than it was in that place of astringent realities we sometimes referred to as "Indian Country." The offensive was well planned, but the man who masterminded it, North Vietnamese general Vo Nguyen Giap, found that the human situation on the ground was more complicated than any human planner could've anticipated. He'd counted on the offensive being accompanied by a general uprising of the people in the South. The uprising didn't happen, and the Tet Offensive, though catching Americans off guard, became a costly failure for the North Vietnamese and Viet Cong.

However, it played differently in the United States. The news media, which had turned against the war, portrayed it as an American failure, and many people came to believe that it was. Because of this, it became the turning point in American opinion about the war.

That brings up the difficult issue of a free press in wartime. Is it in the national interest to allow certain private interests to divide the people against themselves simply for the sake of viewer ratings, profits, and the personality cult of news anchors? And if it isn't in the national interest in a time of war, or perhaps at any other time, then how should it be dealt with?

The problem here, I believe, isn't whether or not Americans should curtail the right to free expression among themselves. The problem lies in our willingness to deceive ourselves about the kind of democracy we have. It may be that it isn't as free as it looks, and neither is the press. I'm speaking here principally of network television news media, though the discussion applies to any form of public dissemination of information which is labeled news.

The Federal Republic of the United States was founded upon a system of representative government. That means it wasn't strictly established as a democracy in terms of citizen participation. There isn't, as a rule, any direct citizen involvement in law making, etc, at least not in the way some of the early Greek city states would gather an assembly of the people for such purposes. Nor was absolute political and economic equality envisioned. Rather, the nation has (politically but not economically) evolved in that direction in the two hundred plus years since its founding, as has the rest of the Western World.

But even if the word democracy is used only to imply some sort of rule of the people in whatever fashion, such as rule through elected representatives, the United States would still, in spite of that qualification, not be fully democratic. Ours is very much a politically limited society.

Nevertheless, it's acknowledged that Americans do vote for their representatives and that their representatives do frame their laws. It's further maintained that, if the people's representatives don't properly represent them, they can be withdrawn, though withdrawing them is neither easy nor immediate. This sounds good so far.

But carefully concealed by the political language of our time is the simple fact that our nation isn't composed of a democratically free people. By the use of the word *democratic* I'm not suggesting that any body of people in social union is free in the sense that each individual can do simply as he or she pleases. What I mean by *democratically free* is that there are no internal restraints other than laws made by the people (I won't speak of the force of opinion or prejudice here). Those laws, in such a case, should be made without coercive influence.

But, alas, upon closer investigation we find the situation to be otherwise. Given human nature and its brilliant use of subtleties to undermine every fact and to cause appearances to stand far apart from realities, this shouldn't be surprising. The reason it *is* surprising is that Americans are encouraged not to think about political realities within certain contexts, and so effective is this prohibition it's hardly ever violated. It seems that, after a long Cold War waged against the evils of Communism, Americans have come to accept the idea that they shouldn't examine their institutions in economic terms, since such a way of thinking might appear to echo the language and rhetoric of the *Manifesto of the Communist Party*.

Marxism (Communism's philosophical name) has long claimed that Capitalist political institutions are derived from the underlying Capitalist economic structure. This is the general view: The type of control exercised over the material means of production determines the relations between social groups, or classes, in a society, and those relations are reflected in the peculiar structure of that society's institutions.

But if this is the case, then it would imply that the majority of the people don't govern in a Capitalist system. It's only those who hold economic power and control the means of production who govern.

I don't wish to trumpet Marxism here, but its tenets can at times serve as a valuable critical tool. Let's ask a couple of simple questions in regard to our discussion of war, its derivation in society, and its relation to a free press. First, when Americans (who live in a Capitalist society) vote for their representatives, how much control do they really have over who the candidates are? And how much public exposure are those candidates able to get independently of private (special interest) financial support in order to gather votes? This is vital, because whoever truly controls the choice of representatives determines what wars will be fought.

We all know that campaigns in this society are funded by "special interests." And we're fully aware that legislation is carefully (though perhaps subtly) proposed over dinner and reviewed in its progress through both branches of the legislature by lobbyists. Our president is elected and influenced in the same way as our legislative representatives, so there's no check and balance here.

At election time in both cases, the people are handed a very small jar of jelly beans. They're asked to pick a few beans from this jar. Of course there're hundreds of beans that never get into the jar in the first place. Having picked a few beans, the people are then asked to vote for their preference among them. That's the selection process. The refiners of jelly bean collections are the special interests. They operate quietly in the background through financial contributions to campaigns. The lobbyists, who work for these special interests, do much in a more personal way to shape the rules by which jelly beans are chosen.

The second question is this: If much of the news media is motivated by vanity and profit, as I mentioned, then how reliable is the information it gives? I don't speak here of facts in themselves. I'm willing to credit the media with facts. But what I'm concerned with is the manner in which those few facts are chosen from a great many, and how they're presented to the viewing public, that is, what tone and context they're packaged in when delivered as news.

Is a press run for profit really a free press? Will it present news on the basis of an objective presentation of information, or will it color the facts to give them drama and a sort of box office draw upon the public? Network television survives by advertising. The more people who see and respond to the advertising, the better. So the more people riveted to the news by a melodramatic presentation, the better for the media. It's a powerful temptation almost never resisted.

It's not only a matter of the news. Something of a cult of personality is also involved. News anchors seem to present themselves for maximum possible public consumption. They're chosen for their looks, the gravity of their voices, the dignity of their presentation. In short, they're performers. As a general rule, they soon become full of themselves and begin to pontificate. That is, they clothe their facts in opinion, like a hot dog wrapped in bacon. All this Americans are exhorted to accept as good, objective journalism. It's for the good of the people that the facts are presented, not raw and indigestible, but with a leavening of experience and wisdom.

If a nation's politicians are controlled by what are now called "special interests," can anyone be certain that their representatives will legislate with the heart of the people foremost in their thoughts? Not at all. Thus that nation's wars will be questionable, and once young, innocent men and women are committed to those wars, they're likely to suffer one of the worst of social crimes. That is, the nation, slowly awakening to its discomfort with the war in question, may decide to turn against them.

So, in the matter of war, as in all other matters, a society should look to the clear-headedness of its thinking. It should ask itself who's in control, because if the people aren't in control, they're, at least, in control of the fact that they aren't.

That means the people of any society that calls itself free—those very people are ultimately responsible, either through action or neglect, for the initiation and conduct of their nation's wars. If such power has slipped out of their hands, or never yet been truly put into them, they can yet shake off their lethargy and condition of sleep to make the necessary changes to restore power to themselves. Otherwise, they're in fact not free, and such a condition raises the ugly prospect of wars being imposed unwillingly upon them.

A free and responsible people needs access to the truth to make strong, accurate judgments. So they should acknowledge this and find a way to free the sources of their news from economic control. At least, they should make sure they have such free sources available. Having accomplished this, the people should then tend to the business of also freeing their representatives from economic control. Unless the people of a democratic society does these things, it's being willingly duped. Either way, it's responsible for the result. War rarely just happens. It's planned—somewhere.

What Is War?

How War Defines Being

The last time I saw our combat correspondent he was gaunt looking with sunken eyes. He'd spent a few months in the Khe Sanh area and had seen too much. A correspondent can get out of a firefight just about any time because he has the same priority as wounded on helicopters, but Corporal Stoddard didn't do that. He used his privilege to go from one hot spot to another.

But that's not the Stoddard I remember. He was easy going, the kind of guy who laid back, took it easy, and wrote news stories about heroic battles we'd been in that none of us ever heard of. Like the time the sapper was found dead, stretched over our perimeter wire in the morning. We took casualties that night, but that one body on the wire was as far as the enemy got. Not according to Stoddard. According to him the North Vietnamese Army broke through our wire and spread themselves all over the compound. By the time we beat them back, there were only a few of us left standing. We read some of his garbage in the Stars and Stripes. Most of it didn't get through because the editors weren't that stupid. But now and then we got a good laugh.

"These gooks aren't human," he told me one night. We were lying on the perimeter answering fire from a Viet Cong probing action coming from a village across the river.

"Yes they are," I said. "They've got feelings."

"Not like you and me. They've been here thousands of years. Have you ever seen a wheelbarrow?"

"No."

"Well keep shooting. You're not going to hit anything human."

One day Stoddard got a letter. His girlfriend was having a wonderful time with someone else.

Tollefson

Three days later we were on hole watch together. It rained all night. We sat on top of the bunker in our ponchos because the inside of the bunker was a pond. I remember sitting there, my rifle sticking up under the poncho and my boots sticking out. The water poured off me, making gullies out of the folds in the plastic. It was cold and all I could see of Stoddard in the dark in his poncho was his face and his wet blond hair stuck to his forehead.

"Shit," he said, and he sat there for an hour without saying anything else.

He didn't have to be there. As a correspondent he wasn't supposed to be pulling perimeter duty. There was a third guy with us but he was asleep. I was imagining what Hawaii would be like if I ever got there on R and R. After a long while the downpour slowed to near a cold sprinkle. It never stopped, just slowed down.

"Ever been to Hawaii?"

"Yes."

"What's it like?"

"Nice."

"What's nice?"

"Doesn't have any gooks. Doesn't have any bitches either. Not anymore, anyway."

"I thought you had to be married to get Hawaii for R and R."

"I'm a correspondent." He smiled.

Stoddard the genius. For a while we sat there in silence. Finally I said, "It's McKenzie's watch."

"Let him sleep," Stoddard said. "I'm not tired."

Stoddard left us during the rainy season and went to the Khe Sanh area. The first time I saw him again he was really gung ho. The Marine Corps wanted to send him home and he was fighting it.

"They claim I was wounded three times," he said, laying out his blanket roll on the hooch floor, folding it, then mounting it on his haversack. He was getting ready to go back and was preparing his pack. Three purple hearts for three wounds and you're automatically sent home. "I was only wounded twice."

What Is War?

He explained that he'd been in a firefight after previously receiving a wound in another one. In this one he got shot in the hand and caught shrapnel in the back from a Chinese Communist grenade. They weren't serious wounds and he insisted they were only worth one purple heart since he got them together.

The Marine Corps must have accepted his argument because they didn't send him home. He went back to Khe Sanh. It was the beginning of 1968 after the Tet Offensive and there was a lot of activity there: Khe Sanh Combat Base and the battles of hills 861 and 881 north and south. He was in the middle of it.

As I said, the very last time I saw him, a few months later, he looked like he'd had enough. And it was only a week after he left again to go on an operation south of Phu Bai that I heard he was in a village with a patrol and tried to enter a hut. A forty-five caliber automatic pistol was facing the door, rigged to a wire. He was killed.

I remember a conversation we had sometime that night on the bunker in the rain shortly after he got the letter from his girlfriend. We'd been hearing about all the anti-war sentiment and protests, so we were discussing our reasons for fighting for our country.

"I'm not fighting for my country," he said. "I'm fighting for the Marine Corps."

* * *

The *Stars and Stripes* is an Armed Forces newspaper, and its contributors are members of the U.S. military. The incident in the vignette isn't a criticism of that paper. But it does attest to the infinite distance that lies between those who're in the battle area and those who aren't. Every Marine has a somewhat raw, and occasionally wild, sense of humor. I don't know how many times I've heard the phrase, "those crazy Marines." It hasn't always been spoken in praise. There's usually a tone of bewilderment in the statement.

Marines enjoy being thought of in this way and cultivate the reputation. This peculiarity can be attributed to their initial acquaintance with the infamous Marine Drill Instructor. A Marine Drill Instructor isn't a drill *sergeant*. He isn't addressed by rank. His name is Sir. I myself, while in boot camp, was thoroughly convinced that my Senior Drill Instructor was utterly insane.

It wasn't a matter of his being mean or nasty. No doubt those epithets applied at times. But a Marine Drill Instructor has a special quality of irrationality that fuses into the brain of every Marine what some might see as a warped sense of humor. That humor becomes a mainstay and sees Marines through thick and thin.

The more widely familiar combat version of that humor, which many combatants in many wars and services have developed, is called gallows humor. Marines get it early, as a product of optimism rather than pessimism, and it was only after boot camp that I came to realize I'd been through the most carefully planned and rational training I was ever to experience. I could understand war because I understood craziness, and we all knew how to move quickly and decisively in the middle of it. It turned out that every bit of insanity in boot camp had a life-preserving purpose.

Corporal Stoddard in the vignette is a product of that culture. His willingness to adulterate his stories is, of course, a reflection of his own devil-may-care character. But the perverseness of attitude in his view of the situation is, in spite of the narrator's remarks, shared by his comrades. Their view is that others have no idea what their situation is, and one story is probably just as good as another in helping people to understand it. Stoddard simply takes this attitude a step further.

Another view expressed by Stoddard is what would be referred to in sociology as ethnocentricity. He sees everything from an American perspective and can't imagine how people could be otherwise. If they're different, they fall short of the definition of what it is to be progressively human. They must not be human.

Of course, it's also not hard to see below the surface of this view. There, in the common ground of all combatants, is the need to dehumanize the enemy. Since killing Vietnamese is what the war in question came down to, it was helpful not to humanize them too much in one's imagination. Even the narrator is aware of this, though he insists on taking the opposing viewpoint.

Finally, we glimpse Stoddard's essential courage in his pushing himself to the limits of his psychological endurance by experiencing as much combat as he can. He does this in part because his cares back home have been extinguished by his girlfriend's abandonment of him. But the Marine Corps is also his world. In addition, he does it because it's an expression of the steel that underlies his apparently flaccid character.

So, what we have here, as mentioned before, is war representing, not life in general, but life stripped of pretension, life as it is. Even Stoddard's attitudes about the uselessness of news reporting (since nonveterans won't understand war anyway) and the inhumanness of the Vietnamese are, in fact, transparent. He's expressing his belief that war is uncompromisingly brutal and that that's the only reality. If others don't understand it or don't measure up to the demands of the situation, that's their concern. His concern is with the reality he sees around him. And that concern is shared by his skeptical comrades.

Life, then, stripped of any falsifying embellishments, is like war, and war's about survival. The sole enduring comfort to be found in that quest for survival is the bubble of human involvement one finds oneself in. That's all we have. I don't mention God and nature here as consolations or forms of refuge because they're expressions of the former two, of life and social belonging. Life, in a word, is simply about *being*, and *being* gets its meaning from our interaction with others. We exist as individuals for the purpose of being part of the human experience. Beyond that there's nothing.

With life up front and war in the background but still on our minds, let's take up the human condition as a whole—the raw human condition, the "naked we came into the world, naked we go out of it" condition. Let's begin with one human being, a single conscious entity. Let's assume free will because, on the one hand, its validity or invalidity can never be rationally determined and, on the other hand, any ethical discussion without it is meaningless. With these factors in mind, we ask, What does it mean to be a human being? (As can be seen, we're getting more abstract here.)

Beyond consciousness, a human being is what he discovers himself to be. That discovery is a complex portrait of himself assembled over time. He finds he's a body among other bodies, living or inert. He finds he has a personality distinguishable in some features from other personalities. He learns a value system from his parents and other social influences. All these things are perceived in consciousness and stored in memory, to be recalled from time to time to consciousness, except where the memories are too painful or troublesome to be permitted to reenter it.

The key here is consciousness. It's a conscious entity that does all this. But in defining itself, that conscious entity both craves and needs other conscious entities of an equal capacity. We can interact with animals, but they won't define us in the way interacting with other human beings can. They don't help to articulate our own sense of ourselves as well as they might because they aren't as smart as we are. So, if each of us is to be anything more than an empty shell of consciousness without the exercise of will, we need other human beings to limit, test, and shape for us the nature of that will, so we can understand it. It's our actions, mostly consisting of reactions to other human beings, that make us what we are.

Out of these two things, a single human consciousness and the necessary plurality of human awareness (more than one human consciousness interacting with others), comes the most essential part of what we call human experience: We're human because we're part of the human group.

Now nature can soothe the human heart. But it can only take this place of importance in our lives because it enters into human experience as an extension, or enrichment, of what we're conscious of. It can never be a center of individual awareness. It can't do this because it's only representative. It's a representation of the sum total of the varied conditions of life, as we perceive them whole and unified in our consciousness.

When we say, I feel at peace in nature, we mean, I feel a sense of harmony in it. That harmony is reassuring and beautiful because it's orderly and purposeful. But where's it found? It's found in the mind of the perceiver. We don't know nature itself. We *perceive* it. It's in the mind. Its final reference is always to consciousness.

Nature can also express for us the orderliness of the mind of God, if we're of a temperament to interpret it in this way. If we do so, it affirms God's existence. But the orderliness itself is simply a mode of perception. It's *how* we perceive. We perceive things as having an orderly connection to one another. This takes place in our consciousness.

God, then, can be conceived of as the cause of the orderliness of nature. He can also be conceived of as the cause of human awareness. We can't arrive at a cause we don't see, so we're left with the orderliness of nature and human awareness. These both belong in the realm of consciousness. So, for all practical purposes, God and consciousness are indistinguishable as experience. Of course, we can add whatever attributes to God we wish. But as raw experience, he's simply an expression of human awareness and all that human beings are aware of. He's consciousness, both the fact of it and its content taken together.

What I'm attempting to explain here is how it is and why it is many of us *do* believe in him. He's an expression of what we are. But, since we perceive our physical selves as not having always existed, our awareness would also appear not to be eternal. So he becomes, for those who wish to believe so, human awareness without reference to mortality. In other words, *we* are *being*, cut off by material limitation. *He* is *being*, unhampered by such a constraint. We, many of us, are driven to embrace him as a means of reconciling the experience of consciousness with the experience of death.

This is the dilemma of every human being. But it isn't generally understood in such terms. Many people seek refuge in religion without much critical examination of themselves, of their motives for seeking such a refuge, or of the tenets of religion. Conversely, men and women who go to war are those who feel a need to return to this stripped down truth of human experience. They want to experience life as it is. Life as simple existence and community. In other words, life expressed as: We exist; we find meaning in community.

Stoddard and the men with him know this, though they'd certainly find it strange to read about it in such abstract terms as are found in this book. To know something isn't necessarily to think about it. For them, that'll come later. It'll arrive in the long, quiet, lonely years after they return from the war and find themselves alone with what they know—those of them who are fortunate enough to do so.

What Is War?

The Demands of War

At Phu Bai the food was terrible. I had been there before and knew about the powdered scrambled eggs that you covered with syrup. The heavy slices of Spam between thick dry crusts of bread were also memorable. All the comforts of home.

This time it was the rainy season and the sucking mud was the first thing I noticed. I had jumped off the back of a truck and sunk all the way to my knees in the muck. It was in this position that I heard over somebody's transistor radio that the war had gotten too tough for President Johnson and he'd decided to quit.

I had come to deliver two prisoners, both young and female. I told them to get down out of the back of the truck. The first one, the round faced and sassy one, flipped me the bird and told me to go screw myself if I could, but she doubted I was man enough. She got down muttering something like "American GI shit!" She was about sixteen. The second one was a little older and badly wounded. She had a hole in her back from shrapnel that was at least a few days old. Our corpsman hadn't treated it because she wouldn't let him near it.

I don't know how she got the wound. When we picked up these "Viet Cong suspects" in the village she was already in that condition. It was amazing she could even get around. I helped her off the truck. The other one said, "You touch Vietnamese woman. You dirt. Filthy imperialists!" She spit on the ground. This is the way she'd been all the way into Phu Bai.

I just wanted to get rid of these two, especially her.
"Where's G-2?" I asked. "Colonel Haskins."

Tollefson

Somebody pointed along the row of tin roofed hooches to a conglomerate of wooden buildings. "Over there. I just came from there. He's down in the COC bunker with the General."

I knew that the Command Operations Center was a big underground bunker dug next to the wooden buildings. As I walked along behind my prisoners, I could observe some of the changes that had taken place since I'd been there a few months before. A lot of the hooches were gone, blown to splinters by rockets. Most of the mess hall was gone too. Only the galley was left. It was noon and I could see a sergeant standing next to the useless door. The seating area to the left of it was gone. Every now and then he'd hold up his hand showing five fingers. A good distance away there was a line of Marines holding mess kits. At the sergeant's signal five of them would approach and pass single file in front of the serving bins. Slop, slop. The different items offered, like green beans, canned peaches and cold powdered mashed potatoes, were piled one on top of the other in their mess kits. They moved away then and five more were called up. It was a slow process, especially in the rain. You could see scattered groups of two or three Marines eating together, some sitting on the ground out in the open weather, others crowded under the eaves of hooches with water running off the tin roofs onto their knees.

Sergeant Dunn in one of the wooden buildings took charge of the prisoners. I went down to report their arrival to the Colonel.

He and the General were in front of the big map in the main room of the command bunker. In a row on the opposite side of the room sat a bunch of office pogues manning field phones. Their one long desk faced the map.

"Sir, Corporal Tennial reporting. The prisoners are delivered. Sgt. Dunn is taking them down to the medical hooch. One of them is wounded. Our corpsman thought the other one might have gonorrhea."

"VC nurse?"

"Yes, sir."

Another colonel, a full colonel, walked in the door just then.

What Is War?

"General Johnson."

"Dave, how are you doing?"

"Lousy, Jim. What's this shit about pulling off the air cover for my men?"

"John thinks we're taking too many hits. He says the aircraft are too expensive for this kind of close in stuff. They're getting all shot up."

"General Jones?"

"Yes. Sorry, Dave. I tried to explain your position. He wouldn't see it my way."

"Damn it, Jim. I'm losing men right and left. First you pull off the tanks because the streets are too narrow and we might damage some sacred architecture, now this!"

"I'm sorry, Dave. You're going to have to go in there and slug it out alone."

On my way back down the dirt road beside the hooches, we suddenly got hit by a rocket and mortar barrage. The rockets came roaring in, one by one, like Phantom jets. After each one hit, there was a loud crack and a boom, everything shaking, shrapnel, wood and tin flying everywhere. Meanwhile mortars were being quietly walked from one end of the compound to the other. They don't seem as scary, so they do most of the killing. Down in a culvert, I was lying on my face in dirty chill water. Two or three rats were running back and forth, one over the back of my legs. They were upset because of the ground shaking and all the noise.

* * *

One of the ugliest circumstances of war is the fact that saving lives won't always be the top priority. Sometimes men are sacrificed on what amounts to a suicide mission for whatever tactical reason. Or, as happened at Bloody Nose Ridge on the island of Peleliu in World War II, men are asked, at a high casualty rate, to go in and do what heavier supporting fire (artillery, Naval gunfire, aircraft) might've done, or at least partially done. There can be a number of tactical or strategic reasons for this. No one would deny that the job of any combatant is difficult, and that the task of infantry is inherently gritty and bloody. It's because of this that I have an unparalleled respect for the infantryman.

But the problem here is that the reasons for such sacrifices aren't always clear. Sometimes they're the products of poor decisions, as may well have been the case in this vignette, when air and armor support were withdrawn to preserve the sacred architecture of Hue. At other times, the reasoning behind such a decision is sound but not understood by those called upon to make the sacrifice. Yet they must "saddle up," "move out," and do what they're told. The obligations brought into existence by a close bond of trust, such as is found in the military, are sometimes weighted a little in the direction of those who must do the most trusting—those who must follow orders.

Another unpleasant condition of ground war in particular, which is part of the reason for my high respect for the infantry, is that they're more likely to look their enemy in the eye, see his mangled corpse, or witness civilian casualties. All combatants experience the death and suffering of their comrades, but generally infantry alone sees these other dimensions of war. Infantry sees it all.

There's nothing antiseptic about ground combat. Nothing is left neatly tucked under the soothing balm of ideals. Everything is uncovered, and eventually everything must be dealt with. Not only the problem of being killed but the problem of killing. Not only the killing of the enemy but the accidental or unavoidable killing of innocents. It's all there, up front, for the senses, heart, and mind of the infantryman.

Prisoners are another challenging feature of ground conflict. What to do with them when troops are on the move or when they need to maintain concealment. Guarding prisoners drains manpower and can jeopardize a mission. On the other hand, killing unarmed human beings, even those who a moment before were the enemy, is distasteful. Is it ever moral?

What Is War?

In a guerilla war, there's the question of detainees. Detainees are usually people suspected of aiding and abetting the enemy. Sometimes they simply *are* the enemy operating under the concealment of civilian garb. It's often hard to tell what they are. So how should they be treated?

The complexities are always there. They're magnified in a guerilla war that involves the civilian populace. All these things play upon the mind and heart of the combatant and strain his nerves, because he's always making decisions about what he can't know. These decisions must be made in the midst of tactical concerns. They often threaten to dangerously modify those concerns.

Is it any wonder then that these troops, even the most disciplined of them, should break down upon occasion and commit atrocities? The most publicized example of this in recent times was the My Lai Massacre, which took place on March 16, 1968. Hundreds of Vietnamese old men, women, and children suspected of being Viet Cong sympathizers were gunned down by members of the Army's 23rd American Division. It was not reported until the incident was uncovered a year later.

The only officer punished for the crime was Lt. William Laws Calley, Jr. His original sentence of life imprisonment was later reduced to 20 years, then 10 years, until finally he was pardoned by President Nixon. These alterations in sentencing demonstrate a sense of confusion on the part of both the public and judicial and government officials as to what should've been done about the case. Many felt Calley was being used as a scapegoat.

So the question here isn't only, What's the right course of action for combatants in each situation? but, How should they be held accountable for their actions? Whose court is the proper tribunal for exercising jurisdiction over what appear to be unlawful acts committed by combatants? The principle cause of the confusion might be stated in this way: Do the legal standards of a civilized society apply in such a case, or does the complexity of a hostile battlefield environment demand other standards? Held against the standards of a civilized community, are battlefield decisions and acts mitigated in some way?

Generally, those laws of a civilian nature that are deemed applicable to a military situation, in and out of combat, are contained in the military code of conduct. But the fundamental question is, Is even the military itself capable of anticipating what might be termed the moral rigors of combat? Can military legal planners foresee the stresses and conditions of new forms of combat not yet experienced by the military? It's generally said that the military is always fighting a previous war.

The Vietnam engagement was in many ways fought under the rules, strategy, and tactics of World War II and Korea. Lacking permanently contested terrain, this approach resulted in the absurdity of body counts. The Iraq situation, in spite of its greater emphasis on acts of terror against civilians, on television propaganda, and on street fighting, is no doubt viewed in many ways in terms of Vietnam.

Even within the same war the situation may vary. The Korean conflict began as a conventional war and ended as a war of attrition (more like a guerilla war in its abandonment of an emphasis on capturing and holding terrain). This latter development placed different kinds of stresses on officers and men than those experienced at the beginning of the campaign.

Perhaps the greatest evil that's likely to occur when an armed force is fielded by a democratic society, comes from the pressure of public opinion upon military decision makers. In a trial for a perceived atrocity, the armed force in question may wish to curry the favor of the nation, especially if things are otherwise going badly for the military.

Under this circumstance, the public's sense of fairness may prevail, exerting pressure towards leniency, as it eventually did with Lt. Calley. As I said, many felt the lieutenant was being used as a scapegoat. But it's also possible that popular opinion will take a harsh turn. Lenient or harsh, the public's opinion is precisely that, an *opinion*, largely predicated on emotions and a confused sense of the facts and situation.

The Many Historical Causes of War

On the morning of Tet at the end of January 1968, the North Vietnamese Army marched into the city of Hue in military formation and took it over. They assassinated most of the South Vietnamese officials who had anything to do with the United States. We found civilian bodies piled into mass graves all over the place. There were no American or South Vietnamese combat troops in the city at the time of the takeover, but there were plenty of CIA agents. They wore civilian clothes and were pretty conspicuous. Many of them escaped out of Hue through the underground sewers. They were brought to 1st Marine Division Forward Headquarters at Phu Bai combat base for debriefing by the General, and it took four weeks for American Marines and South Vietnamese troops to retake the city.

Just before Tet, Khe Sanh had started up and the siege ran on until early April. All these activities produced a lot of captured weapons. But the losses didn't stop the North Vietnamese. Even now as we were carrying the weapons south to Da Nang in a military convoy, there was a bloody fight going on in a nearby mountain valley not far south of Phu Bai. A company of Marines, while in the middle of thick, high canopy jungle, had stumbled unawares into a North Vietnamese regimental base camp. When we left Phu Bai, they had been pinned down for three days with the bodies of their own putrefying dead piled beside them. I had heard a first hand description of the stench and flies over the radio. You could hear weapons firing and feel the fear. Reinforcements were having to work their way in to them on foot

What Is War?

because the jungle canopy was too thick to reach them by air, even to take out the dead and wounded.

It was hot and dusty as always on the slow, winding road that led south through the Hai Van pass on the sixty mile trip to Da Nang. The surrounding hills were covered with short dense brush jungle that appeared to be light green, almost tan in the shimmering heat. We passed some Army engineers working on a part of the road.

"They're up there," one of them said, pointing to the hills. The hills were sunny and quiet. I was riding shotgun in the hard, right front seat of a shock absorber deprived two and a half ton truck loaded with captured weapons, many of them new and still packed in the original Cosmoline jelly. We were near the rear of the long column of vehicles, mostly trucks and a few radio equipped jeeps.

We had only gone a few miles past the engineers when there was an explosion and a black puff of smoke ahead of us. Because the front of the convoy had gone around a curve, we couldn't see what was happening. We were forced to stop. Small arms fire started, and we leapt out of the truck and took cover along the side of the road.

More small arms fire, then nothing. Someone signaled and we climbed back into the truck. As we continued on around the bend, Private First Class Thornton, a thin blond Marine about eighteen or nineteen, who was driving, said, "Must've been a mine."

"Or an RPG."

"Think a rocket-propelled grenade would have made that smoke?"

"If it hit the diesel tank."

When we got around the bend, there were two disabled trucks and one of them was burning. There weren't any deep, wide craters in the road to suggest a mine. Several other trucks were pulled over and a couple Marines were standing beside the road. We slowed. A lieutenant came over to the driver's side window. Not far behind him stood a Marine with a radio, speaking into his handset.

"Keep it moving," the lieutenant ordered.

"Did we get any, sir?" Thornton shouted.

Tollefson

"We're looking." He pointed toward the hills. I couldn't see anybody or hear any shooting.

"What about us?" Thornton added.

The lieutenant pointed to the side of the road a little ahead of us and a good distance from the burning truck. I could see a number of Marines, some standing, some kneeling or squatting. I realized there was a corpsman with them and there were bodies. Whether dead or wounded I couldn't tell at first. It turned out to be several wounded and two dead.

PFC Thornton was in an excited mood most of the rest of the way to Da Nang. He talked continually for twenty minutes about his desire to see combat, which he hadn't done. Then he fell silent, concentrating on the road.

"They never quit," I said after awhile.

"Wish I could've been with the platoon that went in after them."

"I haven't heard anything."

"Yeah."

Going back to Phu Bai was different. We left the weapons and vehicles at 1st Marine Division Headquarters in Da Nang and returned on a C-130 transport plane. They marched us in through the open rear rampway and jammed us in there, in the dark cavity of the plane's fuselage.

"All right, move it up! Belly button to asshole, Marines! Let's go!"

We were jammed so tight we couldn't move. It got hotter and hotter. Sweat poured. It was dark. Finally the engines started. They had long since shut up the rear end of the aircraft. When the plane took off, we fell over, all in one mass because we couldn't move. The rifle or canteen sticking in my ribs was uncomfortable, and if it had meant anything, I would have been embarrassed about my sweat running down onto the guy underneath me.

* * *

What Is War?

Elusiveness, of course, is one of the most fruitful of guerilla tactics. Deny the enemy direct contact as much as possible while continuing to inflict casualties upon him. It can be demoralizing. Or, as in the case of PFC Thornton, it can cause the war to seem as if it's always just around the next bend, never quite in sight, something of an illusion or hallucination. The idea is as old as the Roman general, Quintus Fabius, who used similar tactics against Hannibal in Italy during the Second Punic War.

Fabius employed delaying and harassing tactics, following Hannibal and his Carthaginian army about, cutting off their supplies, and continually camping in the hills near the Carthaginian forces. Fabius' use of the hilly country made Hannibal's cavalry useless, and, at the same time, he would not meet the Carthaginians in open battle. He simply wore away at them, until Rome had time to regain sufficient strength to do more than drive the great general, Hannibal, and his increasingly demoralized men crazy.

A little later during the period of the Roman civil wars, we again come across the long lineage of guerrilla operations. The unconventional fighting tactics of the Roman general Sertorius are described by the ancient biographer, Plutarch:

> For Sertorius was always hovering about, and coming upon him unawares, like a captain of thieves rather than soldiers, disturbing him perpetually with ambuscades and light skirmishes; whereas Metellus was accustomed to regular conduct, and fighting in battle array with full-armed soldiers.
>
> …but Metellus coming up, Sertorius vanished, having broken up and dispersed his army. For this was the way in which he used to raise and disband his armies, so that sometimes he would be wandering up and down all alone, and at other times again he would come pouring into the field at the head of no less than one hundred and fifty

thousand fighting men, swelling of a sudden like a winter torrent.

Not many years before the conquests of Alexander the Great, according to the Greek historian, Xenophon, we see yet another version. Mithradates was a Persian commander who employed hit and run tactics against numerically superior Greek hoplites (heavy infantry). To do this, he used light infantry, as well as mounted archers and slingers who could inflict wounds on the Greeks even as they (the Persians) were being forced to retreat.

There must be many unrecorded instances of this kind of fighting. It's the strategic and tactical equivalent of David and Goliath, and it does a pretty good job of leveling the playing field when one side or the other has superiority of strength.

The unique characteristic of America's war in Vietnam was that it was America itself that hamstrung its own effort. The United States was never willing to invade North Vietnam, which thus served as a reservoir and sanctuary for enemy arms and manpower. I won't launch into a discussion as to why the United States wouldn't invade the North. Such an analysis belongs to the field of historiography. For philosophical purposes, I'll simply say that there rarely is a simple and final explanation for anything in history. This applies especially to wars.

If wars are sometimes considered a form of diplomacy by force, that doesn't answer the question as to why political diplomacy proceeded as or ended in war. Why was the decision to use force made? History is a riddle we're always trying unsuccessfully to put a label on. But what I'm saying is that, whatever their numberless causes may be, wars happen because the practical means for them exist.

Young people ready to serve and standing armies available for use tempt the politician because they make war an easy option. It's also true that the willingness of young people (and sometimes older people as well) to rally to insurrection can tempt the angry and determined would-be revolutionary leader. These conditions are always with us. Poverty and frustration might be a cause of anger and social unrest, and so might a myriad of other considerations. But war, like refined sugar, is made because the canes stand ripe in the field and ready for harvest.

The German philosopher, Georg Hegel, thought he'd come up with a means of examining history's causes, which he expressed in his book, *The Philosophy of History*. Briefly, he suggested what might be called a *spiritual dialectic*. According to this theory, a civilization, or society, develops from a set of ideas, which give it its essential character and structure. He called these ideas the *thesis* of that civilization.

Unfortunately, man has so far proven himself to be incapable of fully grasping the nature of reality. So contradictions to the original ideas, or thesis, set in. These contradictions are the *antithesis*. The antithesis expresses the unforeseen obstacles to a particular social development and the unforeseen inconsistencies in the ideas themselves. In other words, that society has been growing and expanding on the basis of at least some false premises carried in the minds of its people.

So somehow this contradiction must be resolved. A ready example might be the American Civil War, since there was a conflict between the high and humane ideals of America's founding fathers and the existing, much less humane, reality of life in the growing nation, particularly in its southern States. These ideals were the notions of human liberty and individual dignity expressed in documents like the Declaration of Independence and the Bill of Rights. Opposed to them was the practice of human slavery.

When the contradiction of antithesis against thesis is solved, whether by war or by some other means—but usually by war or revolution—a *synthesis* is established, either incorporating the ideas of both the original thesis and its antithesis in a new harmony or replacing them altogether with an idea that transcends them. This necessary theoretical outcome is what Hegel referred to as a dialectical process.

So much for one idea. Along comes Karl Marx. According to his view, he stood Hegel on his head. What Marx (and his intellectual partner, Friedrich Engels) proposed is what he calls, the *material dialectic*. Basically, what's happened is that history's forces have been transferred to the realm of the physical.

According to Marx and Engels, when man first settled down to social living, there was a division of labor and that led to the formation of social classes. These classes were divided into a ruling class that controlled the means of production and a serving class that depended for its livelihood upon those who controlled the means of production. For instance, in early agricultural societies there were landowners and peasants, the landowners free to dispose of their land as they wished and the peasants either legally tied to that land or dependent upon it for subsistence.

Since this resulted in various injustices (those in control have more freedom and get more of the benefits), some form of class struggle would develop. It was usually a matter of the economically, and often politically, disenfranchised population maneuvering to get a better share of the benefits.

Eventually, the situation would be rectified with the establishment of a new social order. But, alas, the new social order would soon be found to be defective. It would inevitably include a new minority which was in control of the means of production, and, of course, injustices would follow, leading to another struggle.

On and on. *Thesis*, the particular social order in question (with thesis representing the interests of those in control), leading to *antithesis*, the injustices and class conflict that ensued from that arrangement (with those not in control heading up the struggle), and finally culminating in a different social order, the *synthesis*. The synthesis, of course, resolved the particular conflict, generally in favor of the rebelling party.

The important point to be noted here is that both these theories seem reasonable. But can we use them to solve the recurring problem of war? No. Not so far, at any rate. But why not?

Before modern times the Greeks, Plato and Aristotle in particular, had the idea that social development was cyclical. It involved growth, corruption, and decay. Say a society was a monarchy. It was governed by a king, a leader who ruled in the interest of all the people. Eventually this king, or his spoiled descendents, would grow accustomed to luxury and privilege. This would corrupt the monarchy and turn it into a tyranny that ruled only in its own interest. So the people, led by the strongest class of them, the well off, would overthrow the tyranny and establish an aristocracy.

Then the same thing would happen. The aristocracy, which originally set itself up to rule in the interests of all the members of society, would end by serving its own interests. It would have to be overthrown by a popular uprising. Democracy (or what Aristotle preferred to call a polity, a mixed constitution of aristocrats and common people) would follow.

Alas, in this ancient view even democracy (or Aristotle's polity) would turn out to be vulnerable. The people would grow idle and undisciplined, the corrupt majority demanding more and more for themselves alone, until finally the evil of a "tyranny of the majority" would fall upon the state. In time a popular leader would arise, sweeping aside this diseased condition and reestablishing a good, one man rule, which, of course, is a monarchy. A classic example of all these changes taking place in the order described can be seen in the history of ancient Rome. That history occurred mostly after the lives of Plato and Aristotle, so it might lend some validity to their ideas.

But other ideas have their strong points too. Can they be right as well? How would they all work together, and how could we go about sifting out a consistent way of dealing with historical events, such as war? The problem here is that so far we haven't figured out how to sort out the apparent run-on and run-together nature of all these processes.

Tollefson

The ancients gave us cycles. But neither Hegel nor Marx were cyclical theorists. They thought human society would eventually arrive at a perfect state. It would become fully harmonious and intellectually comprehensive in its vision according to Hegel's view, and classless in the view of Marx and Engels. Such a blissful conclusion to social events in either case would presumably put an end to war.

So what happened? Why hasn't the problem been resolved in terms of at least one of these philosophical outlooks? (There are other theories, if we need them.) Does this mean these brilliant thinkers are wrong? Not necessarily. It can be that they simply have myopic vision. They're each right in their own way. They do each describe a powerful force in history, but they only capture one of them, because it turns out that history is a dizzying myriad of forces all acting simultaneously. It seems that trying to get an intellectual handle on all these forces spinning their threads together is like trying to weave a thousand tapestries with one loom and one pair of hands. It can't be done.

Listen to the Russian writer, Leo Tolstoy, who wrote the great novel, *War and Peace.* He's disputing another theory, a popular one, which holds that great leaders determine the course of history. Taking an example from nature, he says:

> When an apple has ripened and falls, why does it fall? Because of its attraction to the earth, because its stalk withers, because it is dried by the sun, because it grows heavier, because the wind shakes it or because the boy standing below wants to eat it?
>
> Nothing is the cause. All this is only the coincidence of conditions in which all vital organic and elemental events occur.

He goes on to say:

> In historic events, the so-called great men are labels giving names to events.... Every act of theirs, which appears to them an act of their own will, is in an historical sense involuntary and is related to the whole course of history....

God help us! According to this statement, it would appear that even the people in charge of our world won't be able to end war. That's because no one is really in control. History, as Tolstoy sees it, is an indefinable sea of human emotion, the massive tides of which can never be harnessed for anyone's good, at least not by a single individual who's attempting to act once and for all in the interest of everyone.

But let's assume that every one of these views is right, including the popular one about great leaders, and let's assume the addition of other views we haven't mentioned but which no doubt exist. The point is that, if history operates according to all these forces, we aren't going to get a handle on it ideologically. It'd be like trying to catch a school of fish in one cast of a single hook. Such a fisherman would probably starve. We won't get rid of war this way.

What if those people are right who say that warfare is an instinct inherited from our primitive ancestors? Instincts are hard-wired, aren't they? So nothing can be done about them. But then again, maybe something can. Maybe instincts aren't hard-wired. Maybe they're tendencies, as I mentioned in an earlier chapter. If that's the case, there may be a way to redirect the human heart without denying its needs. But, if we're going to do this, we're going to have to look deep into ourselves. We're also going to have to look at the structure of society to see how fair it really is.

Then, if we can give the human heart a peaceful but deeply honest and fulfilling direction, and if we can get people at all levels of society throughout the world to really care about each other and to act accordingly, we might have a chance. Forming personal practices and social institutions that educate and raise the human heart to the highest levels of purity, sincerity, and fairness with an uncompromising honesty, and creating a society that matches such a heart, just might end war. But that's a tall order, wouldn't you say?

Finding Purpose in the Military

We were always racing down the roads in Vietnam, going too fast because we had the ridiculous idea that if you drove fast enough you'd be on the other side of the mine when it went off. I think in the end more people were killed in accidents than by road mines.

It wasn't just Americans who did this. I had a South Vietnamese Army friend—well, acquaintance—who was killed in just such a wreck. I have an idea what happened because I went into Da Nang with him once to get scrap lumber from the Naval shipyard and to steal a little more from a project some airmen were working on. The Marine guard at the Da Nang perimeter checkpoint, who was the only one present when we passed it on our way back to our units before sundown, told us the Air Force was planning on putting up a small building of some kind nearby, which was where we saw the pile of lumber. When I explained that my Vietnamese Army friend needed it for bunkers, he looked the other way while we loaded the extra lumber onto the truck.

My belief that my friend killed himself with his own driving is based on my memory of riding in with him that morning. He had driven his rickety truck so fast I thought it was going to turn over. And he did that because we had passed up the mine sweep team going our direction. This particular road was mined almost every night, and we went about a mile and a half as fast as we could down the middle of the road in a truck that had no shocks and was filled with choking dust. Why we drove down the middle, I don't know. But we sped along, metal peddle to the rusted out metal floor, until we reached the mine sweep team coming toward us. As we passed them, the Marines looked up through the blinding yellow dust cloud we were creating and saw me. The expression I remember observing on their faces through the swirling dirt was one of disbelief.

When Dong was killed, I was only told he'd turned the truck over. That was all. The rest is conjecture based on my experience of our trip together that morning.

Accidents took a lot of lives over there. Not every man is killed by the enemy in a war zone. People do stupid things or sometimes equipment doesn't work right. I myself had the left front wheel suddenly fly off my jeep and go rolling off into a rice paddy. I was doing somewhere between forty and fifty miles an hour but somehow kept the vehicle upright on the dirt road till it stopped. It was only my insane uncontrollable laughter while I was rolling around in the front seat afterwards that lost me the good humor and moral support of my passengers, a lieutenant and three men from another line company. I can't describe the look on their faces, but it was embarrassing to me.

At Phu Bai I knew of a gun crew that was killed when their 155 millimeter howitzer artillery piece blew up in their faces. And my platoon was shelled one night by the South Vietnamese Army. We didn't lose anybody but we were pretty unhappy. That's how I met Dong. He was the liaison for the South Vietnamese Artillery unit, one of whose batteries had fired those rounds. I happened to be with the lieutenant at battalion headquarters the next morning when he went in to make his report, and Dong was there explaining things, mostly promising it wouldn't happen again. Not that we had any reason to talk. Our night ambush patrols were considered more hazardous than the Viet Cong.

That brings up the worst accident I remember. The second squad was out on such a patrol and came in dripping wet early one morning in a dark, drizzling rain. As they filed into our muddy encampment in their ponchos and helmets, water running off them, faces hanging down and tired, one of the guys in my squad said, "Dave, what happened? Did you get anybody?"

They hadn't. We knew they hadn't because we hadn't heard anything since they left in the early morning hours.

What Is War?

It was just beginning to dawn. Dave looked up and smiled. His full rank and name were Private David Brombeck and he hadn't been in country long. We used to tease him about never having to shave. As he looked up, I heard someone shout to somebody else near where I was standing to break out the C rations for this patrol that was coming in.

Dave smiled and gave Lance Corporal Meyers the bird. "Yeah, we did it," he said, jerking his M-16 up to point it at Meyers. "I got one like..." The rifle went off on automatic and Meyers, hit in the face, fell over into the mud.

Usually the company commander writes condolence letters to the family. I wondered if he'd told them Dave forgot to put his rifle on safety. He probably said something to the effect that "your son Lance Corporal Michael Meyers died bravely in the performance of his duty," which I suppose in its way is the truth.

* * *

When the number of non-combat deaths in almost any campaign is considered, war seems all the more wasteful. There's something especially terrible about a purposeless death. Purpose gives life meaning, and meaning gives life definition, sets it apart in brackets. So, whether the emphasis be on the purpose of the individual or the purpose of the group, this kind of meaning is essential. An accidental death is meaningless.

But why do human beings need this definition as individuals, or why do they sometimes seek it by identifying themselves with a group? In any discussion of war, it should be recognized that group identification and purpose are powerful incentives for drawing people into the military. We sometimes call this a sense of duty or patriotism, but what we mean is that the individual is thinking of himself in terms of the group.

Let me say that I doubt anyone has ever gone to war for a single reason. Human beings rarely do things for single reasons. The human will isn't linear but a complex dynamic. I'll use myself as an example.

Tollefson

Like most young men desiring to see action, I was afraid the Vietnam War would end before I got there. And I was in the Marines for two years before I went. That was unusual in itself at that time.

Not knowing any better, I'd enlisted "open contract" and had been put in supply, a rear echelon job for the most part. I got out of that by having myself sent to a year long Vietnamese language school, which made it possible for me to be attached to an infantry battalion in Vietnam. I was in the headquarters and service company of that battalion. That was the best I could do, but it did allow me to serve under fire.

I was sniped at and ambushed when paying calls on the line units. And the firebases that served, first, as the regimental command post (where I spent a few weeks), and then as the battalion command post (where I spent six months) were subject to numerous night probes, a sapper attack (at the regimental CP), and one North Vietnamese infantry assault (at the battalion CP). Of course, this sort of thing didn't happen every day, but it did occur often enough to save my vanity and satisfy my sense of purpose.

The point I'm interested in here is motivation. Why did I do it? Why was it important to experience some form of combat? The answer is that the very definitions of the words Marine and war couldn't be fulfilled without this requirement, so far as I could see. Not when there was a war going on and most enlistees in the Marine Corps were going to it within a few months after their enlistment.

I'd been raised Seventh Day Adventist, a registered conscientious objector denomination of Christianity. But I could never explain to myself why someone else should take my place in a war. That was one motive, probably one of the weaker ones. Another was that I wanted to be a writer and had become convinced by reading Ernest Hemingway that I couldn't know life if I didn't know war.

Then there was the faint vision of the returning hero that's in the mind of every war volunteer. Of course, that turned out to be a disappointment, given America's eventual disillusionment with the Vietnam War. But I realize even now that if I had it to do over again,

What Is War?

it's one of the few experiences I'm sure I'd repeat, even considering what I now know about the outcome. Good or bad, that war defined me. I can't conceive of myself apart from it. Most people I know who've had such experiences have had their lives defined by them in a similar way.

So, is that why I did it? Was I looking for purpose and definition? Yes, I was, among other things. There was also the experience. There was even a sense of duty. But patriotism I'm not sure of. This nation was never really attacked by Vietnam, and I always felt more like a Marine than an American when I was over there. It was easier that way, given the confusion back home.

In essence, what I'm saying is that the sense of *self* is complex. We first develop a feeling of our individual uniqueness as we gradually discover after birth that our conscious mind is separate from the things it's conscious of. Perhaps more traumatically, we find that the things that are separate from us and help to define us often limit us as well. There's a will in things, not to mention other human beings, and we must contend against it.

Our contending against that will in the world is the discovery of our own will. But will isn't a thing which is ever defined in itself. Will is simply that which decides. But what is it that decides? Our thoughts? Our emotions? Our fears? Our obedience to the will of others? It's all of these and more. All of these at once. Few decisions are made without hidden impulses, forgotten memories of pleasure or pain, rational constructions of belief or of the right thing to do, and so forth, all coming together in what we may think of as a well-reasoned choice. In the midst of all this, there's no evidence of a specific thing called will. Its apparent decision is nothing more than the outcome of these things coming together.

Once we understand that will is a crowd, so to speak, or a collection of impulses, we're better equipped to see how it is that we're so often inclined to submit to a group and let it perform the function of will. The group has an advantage. It's external, therefore clear, composite, and well-defined to our mental and emotional vision.

We go with the group because it lends solidity to our sense of self. It gives it bulk, singleness of purpose, and power.

This is, of course, a compelling incentive for aligning ourselves with the military and going to war. We may believe that, if we do this, we'll have better defined selves, a more secure footing in the world. Since we're individually a scattered group of impulses contained within a consciousness, aligning ourselves with a respected group grants us the dignity of a tested, proven, and recognized purpose. The group can be defined in a way we can never successfully define ourselves. This is because we're conscious of the fractured nature of our inner selves. Even the organizing power of thought is little more than a cover, or screen, for our impulses. The military, on the other hand, works at being as unfragmented in character as possible.

Not all people may agree that thought is the servant of impulse, as I've just stated. There're schools of philosophy which strongly oppose this idea. The ethics of Immanuel Kant wouldn't assent to this position. But (following Kant) I say that, even where a duty is well defined by reason, and where that duty is willingly followed for its own sake in the manner Kant would have, there's a myriad of conflicting impulses secretly contending for and against doing this. How else can one account for a *good* will, as Kant calls it, a *good will* that is *willing* to follow the commands of reason? Certain impulses must've won out over others for one to arrive at a *good* will.

That good will is perhaps more fragile than Kant would wish. He did recognize this to some extent. He described a good will as a necessary component of good character, and he defined it apart from reason. But, insofar as I know, he didn't analyze it to the point of solving the problem it poses. It's easier to speak of the will as something whole in itself, something singular in its character rather than composite, than it is to grasp it in such a way as to get a clear view of what it's fragmented nature is.

I mention these things only to point out a fact—that group identification is a means of *self*-definition. We crave to know ourselves and don't. The group helps us in that regard. It sometimes helps us all the more if that group is the military, because the military operates on the bare, easily recognized and much admired principles of courage, loyalty, and self-sacrifice.

Now, what if a military organization is led by a strong and purposeful leader? How many Frenchmen were willing to follow Napoleon wherever he led? How was it that a nineteen year old Alexander temporarily welded warring Greeks together into a military force that could conquer so much territory in so short a time? It's true his father, Philip of Macedon, set the stage for him by bringing the feuding Greeks under his rule. But it was Alexander who led them to world conquest.

The charisma of these two men was not contained within themselves but in the group, the military organization. It was that organization's glories that drew the loyalties of men. These men didn't follow individuals but a form of leadership provided by those individuals that seemed to define the group itself and lend it purpose. In other words, Napoleon and Alexander were like perspective in a painting. Perspective can give a painting structure and a point of reference for the viewer. Without perspective, the painting can seem unorganized and meaningless. But in the end, it's the painting, not the perspective, that holds the meaning for the viewer.

In short, one reason that war happens is that people seek meaning outside themselves. This can involve an entire nation, as well as a portion of it—those in uniform. Once a strong leader puts everything into perspective, and that perspective happens to be a war footing, there can be war.

The Ruthlessness of War

We knew of movement in the valley and that the Viet Cong were using the village to resupply themselves with rice. So we left one night from our little clearing on a hilltop in the jungle and set up an L shaped ambush near the village. The village lay along the bank of the Vu Gia river. Some of us had the river to our backs; others a copse of brush jungle. There was a trail coming out of the village that passed between us and the surrounding rice fields.

The night was overcast. It was the long bone-chilling drizzly rainy season that comes after the monsoons. But it wasn't raining. Just damp and cold for Vietnam.

"Mark." The Marine next to me whispered, motioning toward someone further up the line. I could see Sgt. Curruthers, my squad leader and the leader of this patrol. But in the dark I could barely make him out and had to strain. I was awake but had been in the same position for so long I was in a kind of stupor. I could make out that he was holding something. Quietly I unhooked a grenade from my shoulder strap. I nudged the guy on the other side of me. He carefully slipped his rifle selector from safety to automatic and nudged the next man.

In the village there had been dogs barking. But they'd been barking all night. Every time someone got up to take a leak, I suppose. I heard what sounded like a faint mumble of voices. I was thinking that I was probably imagining it when suddenly they were there.

Two men on the trail and further back, others. My heart started going like a heavy hammer. Not fast, just hard, and I started worrying that I would have to breathe loud enough to be heard.

What Is War?

The two men had stopped for a moment, looking back. Then they proceeded toward us. They were both carrying Chinese carbines. Carefully I pulled the pin from my grenade and carefully dropped the pin to the ground. My left hand was sweaty. The spoon of the hand grenade lay beneath my thumb.

The two men stopped again, looking back along the trail. The others were coming into sight out of the dark, a fairly large group of them trudging along with heavy burlap bags full of rice slung over their shoulders. The Viet Cong guards were wearing clogs but some of the porters were barefoot. They were villagers.

We would have to take them all. You couldn't discriminate. Two more guards came into sight behind the group of six or eight porters. The porters were bunched up and were acting confused or unwilling. One of the forward guards, close enough for us to make out the irritated expression on his face, said in a low, sharp voice, "Di di mau!" Hurry up.

I saw the sudden swing of Sgt. Curruthers' arm. I threw my grenade. The two explosions were almost simultaneous. Then everyone else along the line opened up.

The grenades had landed among the porters. I saw the two guards in front go down under automatic fire and heard the screams and groans of the porters. I was firing my M-16 now and we all kept shooting as the bodies fell and were twisting and turning, trying to scramble or drag themselves off the path. Behind them the other two guards fired once and bolted. Chinese SKS carbines don't fire on automatic. One of the guards fell on the trail and the other got off into a rice paddy. The field was dry after harvest with no standing water, so he didn't make any noise. But you could see his silhouette against the low horizon of the fields. Several of us stood up and cut him down.

Immediately Sgt. Curruthers got up and we all moved off quickly to another nearby tree line. From there we could see across the small field we'd crossed to where we had been before and where the porters' bodies were still scattered on the trail. We waited a good twenty minutes, never taking our rifle selectors off the firing position.

Tollefson

Normally we would have had them off safety from the time we left the hill, but there had been an accident a few weeks before and Sgt. Curruthers had ordered us to keep them on safety till we needed them.

A small pebble hit my arm. I saw Sgt. Curruthers get up and we all got up. We walked quietly toward our handiwork, close enough to get a good look, then turned west away from the river toward the platoon encampment in the clearing on the hill.

* * *

How does one account for the savageness of war? When everything is reduced to an elemental footing, emotions will certainly become elemental. So, is it valid to say that the end justifies the means?

This isn't easy to determine. In considering the situation in the preceding vignette, a couple things should become immediately apparent. First, the ambush had been set up on a path leading out of the village. If the VC guards and porters had been allowed to pass by, detection of the Marines would've been likely. Also, if the porters had been spared, which would've been difficult in a hail of automatic fire, some of the guards might've slipped away in the confusion. A clean sweep of all was necessary, if it was going to be done at all.

The second consideration is more problematic because it lies in the nature of the troops. Marine ambushes were well known in Vietnam for their lethal effectiveness. Since they were set at night, couldn't be detected, and information as to their whereabouts wasn't disseminated even among allies (the South Vietnamese Army wasn't always considered trustworthy), these ambushes were often feared more than the Viet Cong.

The Marine Corps is an assault force, trained in a "hey diddle diddle, straight down the middle" form of aggression. When engaged, its sole preoccupation is forward movement and destruction of the enemy. The Marine Corps tends to be little concerned with strictly defensive measures. I spent time in the Army after my initial service,

What Is War?

both regular and reserve, in the Marines. I was primarily in the New Mexico National Guard, which included seven months of active duty for training as a radar technician.

While on field training during this Guard enlistment, I observed the construction of foxholes and bunkers that were architectural masterpieces. They were carefully constructed, symmetrical, well designed, and pleasant to look at. I'd never seen this in the Corps, certainly not in Vietnam. A foxhole or bunker was usually a somewhat shapeless mass of dirt, sandbags, and structural supports. It was like the food. Functional, nothing more.

A well-trained, highly disciplined assault force is a necessary component of any military establishment. This is especially true if the power in question (the United States) intends to spread its influence around the world, in small matters as well as big. Capitalism is in its own right a virulently aggressive economic system, which demands plentiful sources of raw materials for its manufacturing processes and requires an ever-increasing access to ready markets for its manufactured goods.

The United States is a capitalist superpower. Its Navy has insured the maintenance of open sea lanes for trade. The Marine Corps is the principal land component of the Naval Department's projection of power. In this way the Corps has evolved into the premier assault force that it is. Much of its work has been done with the sea at its back and heavy fire on its lines. It learned early that in battle there are no permanent entrenchments and the only available option is to keep moving forward.

I say this here to account for the uncompromising deadliness of a Marine unit in action. As ought to be expected, such behavior involving human beings against human beings is apt to produce a lack of the finer sentiments. What we may call "the veneer of civilization" is removed. But what is perhaps most amazing is the fact that, though these finer sentiments disappear in combat, they generally return in civilian life. Former combatants are often known to be the gentlest of men.

Tollefson

Eugene B. Sledge, in his account of the fierce fighting for the island of Peleliu in World War II, describes the level of savagery that front line men can arrive at. In his book, *With the Old Breed,* he says that at first he couldn't sympathize with veterans of other battles who'd grown used to taking souvenirs off dead Japanese soldiers. This sometimes included extracting gold teeth. Such souvenir hunting was usually carried out in a matter-of-fact, routine way during lulls in the fighting. It was devoid of sympathy for a hated enemy, and "civilized" standards of decorum simply didn't apply.

In time, after weeks of heavy fighting and death, his own finer sentiments were dulled to the point that he joined in on the souvenir hunting, short of the extraction of teeth. One day he witnessed a fellow Marine at work, who'd become immune to empathetic emotions toward the enemy. The young Marine was engaged in a tooth extraction process.

The body that had these gold teeth was still alive. The soldier had been wounded in the back in such a way as to lose the use of his arms. The Marine drug him into an open space and proceeded to pound his combat knife into the soldier's jaw to get a tooth out. Needless to say, the soldier kicked his legs and thrashed about. This made things difficult for the determined Marine, so, to speed up the process, he slit open the man's cheeks to better get at the teeth, blood filling the soldier's mouth. This unpleasant scene ended when another Marine came over and put a bullet into the soldier's brain to end his misery.

I've already mentioned that in the expedient, amoral conditions of warfare, empathetic emotions are unlikely to be extended beyond the group to which the combatant belongs. This is especially true if the person encountered is the enemy. But how is it that unarmed civilians, when seen to be involuntarily involved with the enemy, aren't spared? Why aren't they exempt from such a void of feeling?

Furthermore, Mr. Sledge reports that he'd been a recreational hunter prior to the war. Afterwards, he abandoned this pastime. This would indicate the return of a full measure of sensitivity to the sufferings of others. The fact that this sympathy was later extended to

What Is War?

animals shows how far Mr. Sledge had learned the true meaning of suffering from his war experiences. Yet he reported himself to have become insensitive on the battlefield. Why did this later restoration of sympathy take place?

Does the end justify the means? What have military discipline and the terrible conditions of war wrought when men kill without feeling? More importantly, how does this hardening of the emotions into insensitivity later turn into a greater sympathy than had existed before the hardening took place? If man were a machine and the end justifying the means could routinely apply to every situation, we might explain these things as opportune adjustments. The greater sympathy in the end would be an appropriate adaptation to a desired appearance of greater wisdom consonant with age and experience.

But any reading of Mr. Sledge's book will dispel the notion that he was a vain and egotistical man. There's a feeling of sincerity throughout the narrative. Clearly, something deeper must've taken place, something which would account for these radical shifts in outlook. I propose that that something was a result of both the effects of environment and of a combination of the effects of environment and past experience.

If Niccolò Machiavelli shows us, as he certainly does in *The Prince*, that we should look at reality without applying ideals to it, that we ought to observe what people actually do in any given situation, then we should ask ourselves how it is that human emotions can be controlled in this way. First, I would say that they can't always. It takes a certain conditioning and strengthening of character to produce this kind of control. That's what military training and the instilling of discipline are about.

Second, I would submit that when human awareness is conditioned by a displacement of the sense of self into a larger, definable body of people, it allows for emotional adjustments the individual, vulnerable self couldn't handle on its own. Isolation often produces weakness, whereas a sense of belonging enhances one's feeling of importance, thereby augmenting emotional strength.

The savageness of close combat is the result of an adaptation to a kill-or-be-killed world where any misplaced emotion might cause a fatal moment's hesitation to act decisively. Discipline and esprit de corps enhance the sense of involvement in a larger purpose and inculcate the habit of finding one's identity in that purpose. Within the extreme conditions of war, anything outside that identity is liable to annihilation, especially if it poses a direct threat. A dead or dying enemy soldier is simply a muted threat, no less reprehensible for being less threatening. A civilian in the service of the enemy is condemned by association. Any attempt to differentiate further could well be fatal to the person who hesitates.

None of this argument permits the committing of atrocities against unarmed and unaligned civilians. The clearly innocent should be spared. But innocence is a hard matter to determine. In the midst of an insurgency it's almost impossible.

Finally, the reason a larger sympathy can later be so successfully restored in the former combatant is because there's a shift in identity and a removal of the previous threat. The veteran, if he comes home to at least some form of acceptance, finds comfort in the bosom of society. He learns to identify with the larger domain, this enlarged social group where threats to his immediate physical survival have been removed. He goes on about his business in a more relaxed, emotion-freeing way.

But such a person never forgets where he's been, what he's seen. Now able to see it from a safe distance and in larger perspective, he contemplates how terrible it was, and he realizes that he can afford to entertain the notion that it must've been terrible for everyone.

Military Power

Nguyen Van Sung was working in our battalion command post mess hall when I arrived in Vietnam. He was quiet, friendly, middle-aged, over-polite. But then most Vietnamese are, until they get fired up over something. We knew he was getting threats from the Viet Cong, that they were collecting taxes in his village and he was refusing to pay them. He never made a fuss about his problems, just showed up one day without his left thumb. The Viet Cong had cut it off.

His hand was wrapped up in a dirty white piece of cloth covered with dried blood. The thumb was cut off clean between the two joints. You could see the white end of bone and the now dried and clotted blood and muscle. It must've bled like a fountain for awhile. We cleaned and dressed the wound at our aid station and then he went back to work as if nothing had happened. His work in the mess hall involved heavy lifting.

Amid the hot, steamy, greasy smells of the mess hall I watched him one afternoon as he went about his work. It was about three days after he lost his thumb, and he was scrubbing out with soap and boiling water some of the big GI cans that we slopped our food scraps into and washed our trays in. His bandage was soaked. He was outside in the hot sun with another white rag tied around his head to keep the sweat off his face, and there was a short line at the door as some stragglers were going in to get some lunch. They were part of a convoy of Marines that had just brought in some supplies for us.

"Hey, Sung," one of them shouted. "What'd you do with the food that was in the can?"

"I bet it's inside being fixed for us now."

Tollefson

Several of them laughed, the young black Marine who'd made the last remark laughing loudest. I'd never seen this new driver before. Sung smiled, crinkling up the long lines in his face, and went on about his work.

"He doesn't understand," the black Marine said.

"Sure he does. Sung, you got boom boom?"

"Oh, many boom boom!" Sung looked up at the Marines with a big grin on his face. One tooth was missing and some of the others around it were black. "Many pretty boom boom. Pretty good."

"How much, man?"

Sung laughed. It was a standard joke between him and the rest of us. Sung was no pimp, and as far as I know his village had no whores. He was just a hard worker.

That night we were mortared. Just for the hell of it, I guess. There wasn't any follow-up assault. Just a few random bullets fired at our hilltop position from across the river. We lost only one guy. The black Marine. That's why I mentioned him. He was new in country and inexperienced. The mortars came in at two o'clock in the morning, and he had stopped to put on his pants. A piece of shrapnel went through the canvas side of his hooch and into his chest. Must've struck the heart, because he died instantly.

The Colonel was furious. This was the same village Sung was having tax trouble in. It was supposed to be friendly, a secured hamlet. The next day Colonel Williams called Sung into his hooch and had a long talk with him.

About a week and a half later we had a sniper, another young black Marine, imported from regiment.

That night I had sergeant of the guard, and this sniper, John Collins, was positioned on top of a bunker on our perimeter facing the village across the river. He was armed with an M-14 with a scope mounted on it. It was one of those starlight scopes that use concentrated starlight to help you see in the dark.

Because I was sergeant of the guard, I learned a few things. I knew the tax collectors were supposed to visit the village around 1 a.m.

What Is War?

They were very punctual. They got there at exactly one. Just walked in along the village street, three of them. The night was cool and smelled of the river that moved like a black shadow below, and there was one dog barking. Otherwise it was real quiet. A baby started crying but was hushed. Two villagers came out into the street to meet the tax collectors. The street was a narrow dirt road, huts and small, French built masonry buildings on either side. The five of them stood close together in the middle of the street conversing. I know all this because I was looking through the scope at the time. It gave a pale green, dusklike appearance to things but you could see clearly.

"They just came in," I said handing the rifle to John.

Cpl. Collins placed the butt of the rifle securely in his right shoulder. He shifted his long slender arms and narrow shoulders, pivoting the rifle slowly on its bipod.

"See them?"

He didn't answer. His face tensed as he put the scope to his eye and his cheek bone against the rifle stock. He was lying down on top of the sandbag bunker. There was a light breeze and plenty of stars.

"Don't chase the bull," another Marine with us remarked.

"Shut up," I said.

John's face relaxed as we watched the smooth, gradual squeeze of his trigger finger. I could barely see the figures in the village without the scope. Apparently one of them started back toward a hut. That's the one who died.

Sung died too. About a week later. Some Viet Cong came into the village one night, dragged him out into the street and shot him through the head.

* * *

War is an instrument of political will. Among other things, it's about the expression of power. It's one group imposing its will upon another. Its four principal forms are insurrection, invasion, a struggle over resources, and a struggle over spheres of influence. All these forms are based upon a combination of economics and some type of egoism.

Vietnam was part of the Cold War struggle between the United States and Communism over spheres of influence. Those spheres of influence, of course, involved access to resources and, in the view of the United States and its Western European allies, markets. Particularly at stake was the political and economic fate of Western Europe, reposing, for the most part, quietly on the other side of the world.

In the preceding vignette the most immediate economic factor that can be seen easily is the VC attempt to collect taxes from the civilian populace. But those taxes weren't why the war was being fought. Rather, given the fact that there was a war in progress, they were being collected to support the Viet Cong war effort. They were, in fact, being collected for psychological purposes as well.

In other words, in larger perspective, it was a matter of egoism: an attempt by one group to impose its viewpoint on others by whatever means possible. So collecting taxes wasn't just a way for the VC to finance their war efforts, it was a way of getting the people to cooperate. That's a kind of intimidation, a psychological goal. One forced step of cooperation at a time. The old man understood this and refused to submit to it.

The four kinds of warfare are often mixed in various ways and to different extents. When a human being (or group of human beings) seeks to possess some portion of his environment, that's generally an economically induced activity, whether it be resources he's after, especially land, or, more inclusively, the territory that contains the resources. Usually there're other people in possession of these things, so one option is to either exterminate them or shove them aside. The other is to dominate them.

Both efforts have been made throughout history, with a predominance given to the latter, especially where the population in question is large, settled, and complex. An example of the first is seen in the French and English conquests of North America. An example of the second is demonstrated in the manner of Spain's conquest and dominance of Mexico. There were a lot more natives in Mexico, and their civilization was more stable and developed, so they weren't simply pushed aside or exterminated. They were conquered and governed as an underclass.

The nineteenth century German philosopher, Friedrich Nietzsche, describes in his book, *Beyond Good and Evil,* the basis for the egoistic need of one group to impose its will upon another. He calls it a *will to power.* He says:

> ...life itself is *essentially* appropriation, injury, overpowering of what is alien and weaker, suppression, hardness, imposition of one's own forms, incorporation and at least, at its mildest, exploitation....
>
> Even the [political] body within which individuals treat each other as equals..., if it is a living and not a dying body, has to do to other bodies what the individuals within it refrain from doing to each other: it will have to be an incarnate will to power, it will strive to grow, spread, seize, become predominant—not from any morality or immorality but because it is *living* and because life simply *is* will to power.
>
> Exploitation does not belong to a corrupt or imperfect and primitive society: it belongs to the essence of what lives, as a basic organic function; it is a consequence of the will to power, which is after all the will of life.
>
> If this should be an innovation as a theory—as a reality it is the *primordial fact* of all history: people ought to be honest with themselves at least that far.

What Nietzsche is describing is something absolutely fundamental to human nature, something that appears to be instinctual. This may not be immediately apparent when it's hidden beneath the ethical veneer of civilization and its learned habits, but in the expedient, amoral relations between nations, especially in a time of war, it's readily seen.

This "instinct" is nothing more than the need for self-aggrandizement at the expense of others. It's an expression of being. If we're to *be*, we must *be* in terms of what we interact with. Our struggle against opposing wills belonging to other people is what, above all, gives our lives purpose and meaning.

Individually and spiritually, we're potentially as large as our own consciousness. But in the material world of personal limitation, we're, in a practical, material sense, only as large as a *consciousness of us* in the minds of others. The need to expand or protect this is what creates conflict. A large, organized conflict involving many people is what we call a war.

The French existentialist philosopher, Simone de Beauvoir, expresses this succinctly in her work, *Ethics of Ambiguity*. She explains that if a man sees himself as the all, he can't be said to exist, because he doesn't exist for anyone else. He's mere consciousness without external definition. Definition comes from limitation. A chair is defined as much by what it isn't as by what it is. So it is with a human being. We're defined in *this* world as something finite, something having recognizable boundaries. We must have the reactions and acknowledgement of others to create and substantiate these boundaries, to set the limits to ourselves that define us:

> If I were really everything there would be nothing beside me; the world would be empty. There would be nothing to possess, and I myself would be nothing.
>
> To will that there be being is also to will that there be men by and for whom the world is endowed with human significations. One can reveal the world only on a basis revealed by other men. *No project can be defined except by its interference with other projects.* [The italics are mine.]

Every human being senses this and desires not only to be recognized, but to enlarge himself, one way or another, in the eyes of other human beings. It's the felt psychological component in Nietzsche's *will to power*. We want to "grow, spread, seize, become predominant."

Civilization mitigates this desire to some extent. It doesn't get rid of it. Rather, it buries it under layers of decorum and the promise of mutual trust and respect. We put away the need to dominate others (at least in the physical sense), or to seize them or what they have, in order to have the same restraint placed upon those others with whom we live in a community of trust. But outside that community of trust, all is in a state of war or potential war.

The seventeenth century British philosopher, Thomas Hobbes, puts it this way in his book, *Leviathan*:

> ...every man looketh that his companion should value him at the same rate he sets upon himself, and upon all signs of contempt or undervaluing naturally endeavors, as far as he dares, ...to extort a greater value from his contemners, by damage; and from others, by the example. So that in the nature of man, we find three principal causes of quarrel. First, competition; secondly, diffidence; thirdly glory. The first maketh men invade for gain; the second, for safety; and the third, for reputation. The first use violence, to make themselves masters of other men's persons, wives, children, and cattle; the second, to defend them; the third, for trifles, as a word, a smile, a different opinion, and any other sign of undervalue, either direct in their persons or by reflection in their kindred, their friends, their nation, their profession, or their name.

In Hobbes' three principal causes of quarrel we find, first, competition. That's the need to physically extend our dominion over others, or over the things that'll make us greater than they are. The second cause, diffidence, is self-defense, which is resorted to when we detect another about to seize from us our lives, possessions, or reputations. The third is the pure egoism of having others think highly of us, or at least think of us in a significant way, though they fear us.

This third cause exists almost naked in a civil society, only slightly covered over in the interests of fair play, usually by an induced sense of civility and modesty. The first and second causes are more firmly bound by laws for the mutual protection of all. But that doesn't mean they don't exist. They're simply muted to acceptable levels of mutual trust. In war, all these characteristics of human expansion and pride are released in their ravenous hunger, like a lion into a Roman arena.

The material, economic side of war is ultimately driven by egoism, but it takes the form of material acquisition and control, for the obvious reason that we're physical beings and are in need of physical means to make ourselves more powerful. Even when a society such as the present United States lives for its physical comforts, it's still compelled to move in the direction of international preeminence by its sense of reputation, and its unwillingness to let go of this is one of the primary reasons for the world's continuing state of international anarchy. Of course, any other nation in the same position would do the same.

A worldwide and common historical example of the expansion of one people at the expense of another is the takeover of territories already occupied. Europeans did this in the Americas. Mongoloids took over the Japanese Islands from an indigenous Caucasian race called the Ainu. Malaysian peoples seized the Philippine Islands from a pygmy Negro race. Later Spanish colonizers of the same islands dubbed these Philippine aborigines with the diminutive, Negritos.

We can no doubt also remember the forced expansion of Greek, Roman, and Islamic cultures, the succession of kingdoms in the Fertile Crescent before that, the Germanic explosion after the fall of Rome, and modern European expansion of European interests and ideas through colonization. The list is endless.

What Is War?

Mankind has been historically far more often, or at least more significantly and jarringly, in a state of war than a state of civil accord. It's the story of our race. "All is vanity," says the writer of the Biblical book of Ecclesiastes, and so it would seem. Whatever our material and economic purpose, the need for personal aggrandizement underlies it. When individual persons identify their sense of who they are with a particular group and commit themselves to armed struggle with another group, we call this condition war.

War may take the form of insurrection, that is, civil war or revolution. It may become the invasion of one people by another. Or, if that isn't possible, it may take the form of a struggle over resources, or a struggle of influence. Egoism on a national, regional, or ethnic scale lies behind most of this, even when there's a real need for resources, like fertile land for food production (induced by something like overpopulation, crop failure, or dispossession by a prior invasion). Egoism is the destroyer of cooperation for mutual benefit. It lies at the political heart of war.

Tollefson

A Veteran in Society

I'm not sure what civilian agency she represented. I think it was US AID. She was young, fat, blond and either Dutch or German. She flew in one morning by helicopter to see the two thousand detainees we'd rounded up and enclosed in concertina wire. At the time she arrived we were feeding them plain boiled rice cooked in big black kettles over an open fire outdoors. In the near distance, across the Vu Gia river, were black pillars of smoke rising from the villages the detainees had come from.

The helicopter had suddenly and unexpectedly appeared out of the blue sky and set itself down near the large concertina wire enclosure. The young woman, about five feet four inches, weighing about one hundred and forty pounds, got out with a little help, looking clean and fresh as cut flowers. She got out and sank to her ankles in thick, partially dried mud. Her face showed no reaction but it didn't look relaxed. Our battalion Sergeant Major, a wiry, freckled, redheaded Marine with a face dried out and lined by weather, cigarettes and hard liquor, led her over to the enclosure.

"These are the detainees brought in from the villages in the Viet Cong controlled area across the Song Vu Gia," he said.

"Yes, I know. How long have they been here?"

"Some for two days, some one, some still being brought in."

"Any sick?"

"Malaria, tuberculosis, dysentery..."

"Awful." She was looking now over the treetops toward the black columns of smoke. The ground shook occasionally with the sound of bombs, and American jets could be seen diving down and rising back

What Is War?

up into the clear sky. It was a bright sunny day except for the black smoke.

The Sergeant Major got a glint in his eye. "Beautiful day," he said.

"Awful!"

A group of the detainees, some old men and a number of women and children, were squatting on the ground eating balls of rice with their fingers off paper plates we'd supplied them. They were squatting on their heels and could sit for amazingly long periods of time like that. All were silent and had blank faces with the stares of those who've lost everything.

The AID woman finally looked away from the burning villages. "We have facilities for most of them at the Nguoi Viet compound in Da Nang. What have you done with the worst cases?"

"They were medevacked out by chopper to the civilian hospital in Da Nang this morning."

"And these are being fed rice?"

"Yes."

"A strict diet of rice?"

"Yes."

"Awful."

"That's what they eat. We haven't been getting any complaints. Would you like to speak to any of them?"

"No!" Her response was almost a recoil.

The Sergeant Major smiled. "Out here you get used to the conditions." He looked at her feet, the chubby white ankles spattered with mud.

There was a sudden commotion of rumbling and creaking. A tank appeared in a cloud of yellow dust and roared past us at thirty miles an hour, then continued on down the hard packed dirt village road, which was already dry after the recent rain. The top of the tank, an M-48 with a 90 millimeter gun, was covered with infantrymen.

"They're certainly in a hurry," the woman remarked.

"Firefight in the next hamlet down the road there." Now that he mentioned it, you could hear the sporadic small arms fire.

Tollefson

"More prisoners, I suppose."

"More bodies. Maybe some of them ours."

"Awful."

The Sergeant Major contemplated her for a moment as one would a stray dog eating something unsavory.

"I will make my report," she said. In the background was the high pitched whine of the helicopter as its rotors slowly began to turn. She turned around and started to trudge toward it. A crewman hopped out and helped her aboard. The Sergeant Major remained standing beside the concertina enclosure. He took out a cigarette and lit it. The helicopter lifted off with her in it, rose into the sky and went away.

An American two and a half ton truck pulled up. Several Marines hopped down from the open rear end of it and began pulling large burlap bags full of rice off it. They dropped one and it burst, the clean white grains pouring over one another out onto the ground. The ground was dry and dusty here near the road. The only mud was in the area around the enclosure, which seemed to hold moisture after a rain longer than anyplace else.

As soon as the bag hit the ground, local village women came out of nowhere, scrambling on hands and knees in the dirt, fighting over the grains, bickering, weeping and shouting, scooping both dirt and grains into their conical hats and the folds of their blouses. The Marines stood and watched.

* * *

In this vignette two worlds stand before us: that of the military and that of the rest of the human community. When no longer a part of the military, a war veteran remains a visitor from one world to the other because, however successful he may be in later life, he can never fully reintegrate into the civilian environment from which he came and to which he's returned.

This is ably represented in Erich Maria Remarque's novel, *All Quiet on the Western Front,* and in much of Ernest Hemingway's work, particularly the short story, "Soldier's Home." In this story Krebs, a young Marine, has returned from service in France during the First World War and finds himself unable to fit back into old routines and associations. Time will no doubt ameliorate his sense of alienation, but it won't erase it, and the reader recognizes this in the story. A similar point is made in Remarque's novel, but the protagonist dies before the war ends. There's a reason for this phenomenon being stressed in these works, and it's pretty much already been given in an earlier chapter of this discussion.

It's this: war cleanses the soul. When I say it, I'm not making a moral statement. The cleansing is more like that of a baptism by immersion, in which the supplicant unexpectedly drowns and is later revived on the bank of a river. Each individual gathered about him, no doubt in surprise and shock at the unfortunate accident, thinks only of his or her own good fortune in that the drowned man has been returned to life. But the revived man doesn't see this.

He looks up at the gathered faces in bewilderment, his vision momentarily fogged. He doesn't recognize anyone. But as recollection returns, he tries to speak of what he's experienced. No one understands. These old acquaintances are then looked upon as though through a veil.

That veil is the difference between his memory of what's just transpired under the water, and the void that exists in the recollection of those who weren't down there with him. In later times, no amount of routine, togetherness, and living under the same social laws can alter the clarity that's attended his life. This is because that clarity had been a clarity of not having seen, followed by seeing.

I don't want to attribute extraordinary qualities to any war veteran, and certainly not a superior status. He's an ordinary person made more ordinary, not unique, by his contact with death. In this, he's of no more importance than someone who's survived an earthquake or a tsunami. But the layers of comfort that once made his life artificially easy and acceptable have been forever removed.

What's more, the horrors he's witnessed were deliberate. They were brought on by personal choice. They weren't an act of nature, over which a human being has no control. On the contrary, that person has himself been a participant in the forces of destruction. For this reason, he knows the responsibility for what he's seen is his own, and he must carry that knowledge with him for the rest of his life.

This is why it's important for a society to accept its veterans and what they've done. Their burdens are great enough, and they were taken on for the sake of the society. It was the society that asked for war.

From a combatant it's reasonable to expect disciplined behavior, not wanton destruction, atrocities, and the like. But what must be borne by the society as a whole is a recognition and acceptance of the inevitable violence that's an integral component of war. There's, however, no obligation in this to overlook any deliberate and cruel harm done to innocents.

The outcome of any war is a separate issue from its prosecution. If the war is won, there's no burden on the shoulders of those who didn't fight it, other than the loss of loved ones (admittedly no small thing in itself). But if the war is lost, the nation must confront its own complicity, its weakness or folly. It's damaged itself and its young. So it must sort out the moral dilemma of having chosen to go to war in the first place, of having chosen to abandon morality, or at least a semblance of that bond of trust that purports to exist between nations at peace.

In performing this task, it shouldn't choose to displace its responsibility for the war onto the veteran. Combatants do fight wars, but they don't create them. If a society disowns its responsibility for asking its men and women to fight for it, there'll arise a division in that society which will be a division at its heart.

After the Vietnam war this occurred. Over thirty years later, it still lies buried in the American soul. What kind of division am I talking about? I'm talking about the kind of division that doesn't let a person see clearly into his own motives. Or a society either. The Vietnam veteran, as a result of intense social rejection, tried not to look into his own heart to sort out memories. He wanted to forget them. The rest of society did the same to avoid recognition of its motives. Neither succeeded.

In other words, there was a breach of trust all around. People learned to trust each other less. They learned not to trust themselves. Confidence failed. Purpose became unclear. In short, the single organism that's a well-bonded society became many separate organisms. That's the price of any breach of trust.

Remember the Biblical story of David, the king of ancient Israel? He desired Bathsheba, a married woman, and wanted her for his wife. Bathsheba was married to Uriah, an officer in David's army. Uriah was a loyal and good soldier, however indifferent he might've been as a husband. Nevertheless, David secretly ordered that Uriah's comrades should desert him in battle, leaving him to the mercy of the enemy. He was killed.

It was an almost unprecedented act of treachery, violating the natural bond of men in combat, as well as the loyalty of a soldier to his commander-in-chief and vice versa. It was murder as well as treachery. These are the things for which David was punished. Killing and betraying. He wasn't punished for adultery, though the prophet Nathan accused him of it. This was because the adultery of deliberate conjugal neglect had already been committed by Uriah prior to David's offenses. Uriah had thus himself previously annulled the marriage bond of trust he'd entered into with Bathsheba.

David and Bathsheba's first son died because death (in the form of murder) had been introduced by them into the spiritual, moral, and psychological reality of their own lives. What they were willing to do, they should be willing to receive. But their second son, Solomon, went on to become Israel's most glorious king. That's not a punishment for an illegitimate marriage.

Nevertheless, Solomon did turn away from the spiritual practices of Israel, thus violating the nation's idea of itself as being in union with God. His behavior also divided the people. That idea of a nation in union with God had involved the practice of reverence for a God especially concerned with the welfare of Israel and had been the unifying ideal of the nation. Going against it was the kind of treachery that'd originally been sown into Solomon's heart by David's example and practice. That same treachery grew in the soul of the nation. After Solomon passed away, it split the country into two kingdoms, which remained divided until each kingdom, growing continually weaker and more divided within itself, was eventually overthrown.

Prior to Solomon's apostasy, David's older son, Absalom, had revolted against his father and had been put to death against the king's orders through the disobedience of David's most trusted general. Treachery and murder were everywhere. It went on and on because the king's household and the nation itself had lost their cohesive bond of trust and the singleness of purpose that comes with it. They'd lost this bond through David's original act of treachery, his initial breach of trust.

I mention this story because it illustrates that a breach of trust can shatter the foundations of morality. So much is this the case that the principle of trust itself is more important than any particular rule based upon it. This is because the specific nature of an individual rule is essentially a reflection of time and place, of historical and economic circumstance. But in trust lies the universal grounding of every society in terms of its human relationships, from marriage to the family to the nation.

In war or peace the most important thing for any society to preserve is its spirit of unity through mutual trust. Oneness in individual custom and practice creates this singleness of purpose in the nation. Within that oneness, there can be disagreement. But when treachery is introduced, when civil accord is ruined by an open breach of trust, it's hard to bring things back together again.

Good Logistics and Spiritual Fortitude

Ham and eggs. A C rations Ham and Eggs is the caviar of foxhole life. It comes in a little olive-green can a couple inches high and about two inches across. You open it with a tiny can opener half the size of a quarter. The opener folds up for convenience and several of them come in a case full of C ration boxed meals. The cans are in the boxes. Some of the others contain fruit like pears or peaches, bars of chocolate and hard crackers that are built to last. But it's the main meal, like ham and eggs, that is a hallucinatory experience. It comes out of the can in a single slippery glob, like oiled Spam, that keeps the round shape of the container. The ham and eggs are perfectly blended and indistinguishable. The meals can be heated in the can with little dry pellets that burn clean and hot. But why bother?

Bathing in Vietnam was a kind of exhibition of naked male bodies. We went down the hill from our firebase in the sunlit evenings, stripped off our grimy, smelly jungle utility clothes and stood in a line in front of a thin horizontal pipe. The pipe extended from a little fiberglass water gathering pool that was set up beside the slime-brown river. Water the consistency of syrup was pumped out of the river, purified in the pool, and shot through the pipe, which had little holes all along its length. The water squirted out the holes and onto the line of naked men. The water was almost freezing. The evening a little cooler than the day, but not much. It felt good when you got used to it. We scrubbed the dust and stickiness from our arms, legs, faces, groins and armpits. I don't know what the young women and girls

Tollefson

thought in the village on the opposite bank of the river. If they noticed, they were discreet.

We retreated back up the hill and inside the perimeter wire after the bath, as the sun began to go down. The nights were generally muggy. We globbed on mosquito repellent. Some of us slept on cots, others in foxholes on the perimeter. In this way we began preparing ourselves for the next day's bath even before the next day started.

In the morning we went down with five gallon GI cans to get more water and lugged them back up the hill. There we washed our faces and shaved out of our steel helmets. We also washed our clothes with that water and a scrub brush. This meant throwing away underwear, since it was just something more to wash.

A Marine's best friends are his suede jungle boots. They are not originally suede but black leather. But it's a mark of not being in the rear echelon somewhere to possess them. I wore mine proudly and carefully cultivated their worn out look. A hole or two in the canvas tops was especially nice.

I'm describing this because these conditions weren't really unpleasant. It was a matter of living simply. I have never lived any better, though I've lived more indulgently.

On the other hand the war deprived the Vietnamese peasants of many of the basics of life. There weren't any fat Marines, but there weren't any weak ones either. The Vietnamese, with their farming methods disturbed, often had little to eat. We were clean. Their children were often covered with sores. I can give a couple examples.

Once we discovered a baby in a nearby village, whose parents had been killed by American artillery. The aunt and uncle were supposedly taking care of it. But they had little food and couldn't spare any. The baby was less than a year old and was only small bones with muscle wrapped around them like dry cords. It had glazed eyes, when open at all, that looked like a dull blue-gray mucous. We took it away, but it died the following day, too weak even to cry.

We sometimes supplied medical help to this same village. We would send a corpsman, and I went along as an interpreter. We set up *under a tin roof extending like an awning from an old French colonial building. The people lined up, including many children.*

"Toi bi hong." I have a sore throat.

We gave them mostly placebos. Fake shots and worthless pills. But we did take care of wounds. And there were often plenty of them from the previous night's fighting, which usually somehow centered itself in the middle of the village.

One woman came to us carrying a small boy in her arms who had fly infested sores all over his head. Yellow puss and black knots of flies. It made you sick. We told her to go wash the kid in the river. She panicked and refused, not understanding that we would use antiseptics immediately afterwards. So we did it ourselves.

One more example. We had a doctor with us one day. A woman eight months pregnant arrived and wanted to be examined to see that all was well with the fetus.

"I'm not that kind of doctor! Tell her!" the doctor ordered me in a panic.

She insisted. I smiled. The corpsman kept a straight face. The doctor, a Navy lieutenant, was his boss.

In the end the doctor took the woman into the building and did whatever he had to.

* * *

It's commonly been said that an army travels on its belly. That's a succinct way of pointing out that the practice of war rests upon an economic foundation like any other collective human enterprise. We couldn't build cities without an infrastructure that fed and clothed their inhabitants. Nor can a military campaign be carried on without beans and bullets. Logistics isn't the most glamorous part of warfare, and it doesn't attract the most adventurous. But poor logistics will defeat an army as surely as firepower, weapons, tactics, or superior discipline and leadership will bring it to victory.

Tollefson

Good troops know this, but they also know that an ability to strip down to the bare essentials and to endure privation, short of producing physical weakness and mental confusion, are among the highest military virtues. The tone of the preceding vignette is such that it's plain the narrator takes great pride in showing indifference to a few discomforts, making a joke of them. These discomforts of his aren't extreme, and far more has been endured by combatants throughout the millennia.

But what's significant here is the narrator's respect for the Vietnamese peasantry and what they stoically endured. This same respect was echoed in the vignette on rains and flooding. What isn't mentioned is the enemy, the North Vietnamese Army and the Viet Cong. The Communist movement in Vietnam arose from the stoic Vietnamese peasantry. They (most of the Viet Cong by this time were from the North) endured unbelievable hardships and bombing just getting to the south. They tended to travel light, requiring little for self-maintenance and making do with inadequate weaponry. They also accepted staggeringly high casualties, expecting with quiet determination to receive only the most primitive forms of medical assistance when severely wounded.

Standards of living. These define a people. They also define an army. Every combatant loves a hot meal, a bath, and at least a few of the other amenities of life, when these can be obtained. But there's nothing more insulting to him than the idea of being given a hot meal the day before an expected battle with the specific idea in mind that he's a mindless beast who needs only to be physically gratified to be content in any situation.

Logistically, armies may travel on their bellies, but good soldiers are carried forward into battle by their hearts. Facing terrible withering fire, as in the amphibious assaults of World War II or the meat grinder of the Battle of the Bulge, or enduring the unseen deadly surprise of modern guerilla and terrorist warfare—these things aren't accomplished by the body alone, but by the spirit of the individual fighting man and the cohesiveness of his fighting unit.

What Is War?

Never say to a good soldier, Marine, airman, or sailor, we fed you well. We gave you creature comforts. If these are available, all well and good. Why refuse them? But when they aren't available and the mission is carried out faithfully, then the true spirit of the combatant shows forth. So rather say to him or her, we had faith in you. We knew that somehow you would hold up through hell for what you believed, and we trained you well.

Strong training and faith. These are the ingredients of strong men and women. Once again warfare becomes a metaphor for life, because strong training shouldn't only be physical and technical, but moral as well. Values are what a stout heart clings to when all else fails. Values engage faith, and faith supports that last exertion beyond endurance, when the effort is most needed.

Faith then has another dimension. It's not only a relation between individuals or between an individual and a group. It's also something else. Faith is a relationship between a person and his or her existence.

When faith exists between one individual and another, or between an individual and a group, we call it trust. But when it's between an individual and his existence, we call it faith. Faith is an expression of *being*, that is, of existence itself.

Where there's free will, possibility and choice will also exist. Since a moral decision is a responsible act, we must assume free will in any moral discussion. (The emphasis here is on freedom, not on the nature of will, which was discussed in an earlier chapter.) Without a free will we couldn't be held responsible for our acts. It's for that reason that we embrace possibility and choice. Simply put, this means that, in any given situation, the individual can chose to act in more than one way. He'll be responsible therefore not only for his choice, but for the consequences of it as well.

Yet he can't control the consequences of his choice. Once his choice is made, it becomes an act, forever stamped upon the reality of this world. Even if the individual were destroyed before he could act, the decision made would've modified his character in a particular direction, and that would be an act in itself. It would've shaped the reality of his character.

But consequences lie hidden in a mist. We see them only partially, reasoning about our choices and hopefully predicting their results as best we can on the basis of incomplete information. In the end, we don't know how they'll attend us. In other words, we don't know the outcome, the feedback, of our actions, or, more specifically, of the decisions which produced those actions. Consequences come to us like thieves in the night. For this reason, we prefer to commit ourselves to acts the results of which appear to be at least somewhat predictable. It's safer that way.

But faith, by its nature, isn't in the business of keeping one's feet on firm ground. That's calculation. People take *calculated* risks when they want to insure their own safety or well-being, physically or morally. They step where they think they can see there'll be firm ground. But even then, they don't know the firm ground is there until they take the initial step, when it's too late to turn back. That's risky enough.

But faith goes further. It *creates* the firm ground. This is the ingredient that's behind all the great achievements of mankind. With these, there's a stepping into the void, knowing it's a void, but trusting one's step will be met nevertheless with firm ground. That's faith.

Socrates had faith. He created a new, ethically rational world. Jesus had faith. He made the individual human heart the dominant force in the expression of a personal existence. Newton had faith. Einstein had faith. The list goes on.

When he died for his beliefs, Socrates didn't know with any certainty that his impact on the world would be what it was. Jesus refused to turn back from the shame of the cross at a time when no one really understood him. (Does anybody now?) Isaac Newton and Albert Einstein assumed the precise nature of physical phenomena that had yet to be experimentally verified.

Did Newton verify what gravitation was, as opposed to what it did? No. He put his faith in measuring its effects. Had Einstein personally measured the curvature of light in a gravitational field? No. That was left for others. But he did accurately predict it.

These men had faith, and many notable women have also joined the ranks of such men, bold women, such as Teresa of Avila, Joan of Arc, Jane Austen, and Emily Dickenson, each stepping into a void and creating a world where others saw nothing. They lived by strong values that were made real for us by their faith in them.

Eugene Sledge describes the tremendous fear and doubt that attended him before the bloody Marine landing at Peleliu. But he went on to do his duty. In *The Red Badge of Courage*, Steven Crane's hero, Henry Fleming, learns by experience that he must focus on his courage, putting his values forward, keeping his mind firmly on the objective, while holding his hesitant and doubting imagination in check. In this way he could finally brave the fire of battle, which made him an effective fighting man. It made him such a man because it made him a complete human being. He'd learned to create himself, having given himself firm direction and an absence of confusion.

Our lives are defined by purpose. Purpose is set forth by values. Values, once we've embraced them, become possibilities, or options, we've chosen. These values are sustained by faith. We can act on them because we chose them. We believe in them. This is the combatant's creed. It's every person's creed. It settles us into what we are and establishes our being. We *are* what we choose, what we do, and we're defined by how we do it. The greater the risk, the greater the faith that encompasses and sustains it and the bolder the definition we've given to ourselves.

Tollefson

Casualties of War

The stench was something awful. I tell you, never dig a man up after he's been dead for awhile. I don't know how the villagers finally found him or where they got the stuff to put in your nose to keep out the odor. It was a matter of one thing stinking enough to overpower the other.

He was a South Vietnamese Regional Forces soldier and had been out with some others on a joint patrol with American Marines. They had been ambushed and somehow in the firefight he'd been separated. It was thick, low growing jungle brush country. Hard to see, and they were in some kind of a swamp near a banana plantation. After the Viet Cong pulled back they never found him. His name was Mien Ngoc Chau.

His wife discovered through the village grapevine that he hadn't been taken prisoner but was dead. One of the strangest things in Vietnam was the way the villagers knew what was going on on both sides of the war. But they didn't know what had been done with his body. We searched for weeks, thinking he was still alive at first and checking the hospital in Da Nang. We thought he might have been one of the wounded medevacked by helicopter. Then his wife told us what she'd learned, and there wasn't anything we could do until the villagers themselves located the burial site.

It turned out that, just as we'd thought, he had been only wounded at first and had been medevacked by one of our choppers to the Vietnamese Hospital in Da Nang. Never mind that the hospital officials didn't know he'd ever been there when we checked. Their record keeping was on the level of their sanitation.

What Is War?

We supplied the truck. The driver, myself and another Marine went with a handful of villagers, including the wife and the man's father, to retrieve the body and bring it back to the village for proper burial. We went all the way to Da Nang and out into the sand dunes. He was buried in the sand only a few feet down in what looked like an oversized orange crate. When we uncovered him, he was bloated and resembled a very fat little man with his legs folded up under him to get him into the crate, which was too small. He really stunk. His skin was stretched tight with the swelling of decomposition and was hard, brittle, dark, almost a burnt orange color, and shiny in the bright sun like plastic.

Bright sun on white sand. This guy smelled really bad. I was trying to help several of the villagers get him out of the hole when I heard a scream. I turned around and his wife was headed right for him. She was going to jump into the hole with him. Ugh. He probably would have popped. I tackled her and with the help of one of the village men dragged her back to the truck, which was parked about thirty yards off. Ngoc Chau's father was squatted on his heels beside the truck, drinking a bottled orange soda. He said something in Vietnamese and she squatted beside him, holding herself with her arms crossed over her chest and shoulders, rocking and moaning. Her long black hair glistened in the white light. The old man kept talking in a low voice, almost a moan himself. There were tears on his dark crusty old face. He never once looked in the direction of the makeshift grave while we got the body out, put it into a decent coffin and loaded it onto the truck.

On the way back the wife was quiet. She sat by herself in a corner of the bed of the truck with a blank look on her face. The old man moved over beside her, and they both sat there without saying anything all the way back to the village. The other younger men talked and laughed, making jokes with me and finishing off the pop we'd gotten in Da Nang to replace the river of sweat that was now covering us with a layer of dust as we rolled and bumped down the road. I was in the back with the villagers because I could speak Vietnamese. The other Marine and the driver were up front.

After we'd dropped off the villagers with their cargo and helped the wife down off the truck—I never saw her again—we returned to our hilltop firebase. As we entered the compound, we came upon a group of villagers. Some were standing, others were gathered in a semicircle, squatting on the ground. As soon as we stopped the truck, I went over and had a look.

The night before we'd been mortared and some of our own counter-mortar fire had landed in a nearby village. That was where the VC mortars and small arms fire were coming from. There had been civilian casualties, and that's what these people wanted: compensation. We usually shelled out money, called solatium payments, for our accidents. But the ones who brought the bodies to us were never the immediate next of kin.

Several of the women—they were all women—were keening. The ones who were squatting had set a straw basket on the ground in front of them. It looked to be full of banana leaves. When I walked up, they pulled the leaves back, uncovering the cold body of an infant. His skull was gone at the level of his eyebrows, leaving a jagged edge all the way around. What was left of his head was hollow inside and the blood was dried to a kind of dark purplish brown. It looked like an inverted plum.

* * *

The problem with civilian deaths in war is the apparent purposelessness of them. I say apparent because in modern warfare, both the conventional and the unconventional kind, civilian populations are routinely affected. This is due to their involvement, whether willing or unwilling, in forwarding the war effort. Civilians are often caught in the crossfire between contending forces, and occasionally, because of their direct involvement, they're deliberately sought out for destruction, as in the fire-bombing of Cologne in

What Is War?

Germany in World War II, or the occupation of Hue City in 1968 by the North Vietnamese Army, followed by that army's systematic slaughter of thousands of civilians judged to be supporting the American and South Vietnamese war effort.

Let me put it this way: Is it in the nature of this world that good and evil people are rewarded according to either their dispositions or their actions? Do the good receive good in return? Are the evil always punished? I ask this because, as I've mentioned before, war strips life to its barest essentials. Let me reiterate a central point in this: War doesn't change the paradigms of life, it merely sets them in bold relief. Therefore it shouldn't be surprising that the innocent suffer. They always do, whether in warfare or out of it.

I'm not condoning deliberate cruelty here. Rather, I'm putting the human heart on trial. I'm saying that such is the nature of the *divided soul* in every man and woman that evil is inescapable. No matter how rigorously we apply rules of justice, fairness, and mercy, we repeatedly misinterpret or fail in them. It's for this reason that we fall short in war of consistently protecting the innocent. We fall short everywhere, in or out of war.

Divided souls? What do I mean by this? Allow me to borrow a couple of illustrations from the Gospel of Mathew in the Christian New Testament. Jesus speaks of tares (weeds) and wheat and how the tares must be left to grow among the wheat until the day of judgment, when the two will be separated. Again, John the Baptist describes Jesus as the one who will separate the wheat from the chaff and burn the chaff while preserving the wheat.

The usual interpretation of the first of these statements is that the weeds are bad people and the wheat plants are good people. The same interpretation is often applied to John's words. The chaff are the bad guys, the wheat the good. Simple enough, don't you think? You'd better pick the right horse if you want to win this race. But there's a problem with this interpretation. Left at this level, it's simplistic. It largely ignores the complexity of human nature.

Another way of interpreting these statements is to assert that both conditions exist in any one individual person. In time, the evil *spirits* (conceived of here as *states of mind*) will be removed. Only the good will be preserved in human nature. But the problem with *this* interpretation is that it says nothing about "just deserts." Even the English philosopher, John Stuart Mill, confirms in his essay, *Utilitarianism,* that just deserts are an essential ingredient in our notion of justice:

> ...it is universally considered just that each person should obtain that (whether good or evil) which he *deserves*; and unjust that he should obtain a good, or be made to undergo an evil, which he does not deserve. This is, perhaps, the clearest and most emphatic form in which the idea of justice is conceived by the general mind. As it involves the notion of desert, the question arises, what constitutes desert? Speaking in a general way, a person is understood to deserve good if he does right, evil if he does wrong; and in a more particular sense, to deserve good from those to whom he does or has done good, and evil from those to whom he does or has done evil.
>
> [This sentiment] is a desire that punishment may be suffered by those who infringe the rule. There is involved, in addition, the conception of some definite person who suffers by the infringement; whose rights...are violated by it. And the sentiment of justice appears to me to be, the *animal desire* [my italics] to repel or retaliate a hurt or damage to oneself, or to those with whom one sympathizes....

The important point, for this discussion, is what Mill calls the "animal desire" to set the record in balance. An eye for an eye and a tooth for a tooth. It stands at the heart of any notion of justice. Of course, that's only to state the negative part of the formula. People should receive good for the good they do as well. The operative word

What Is War?

here is *should*. Morality is prescriptive. It's normative. It talks about what should be, not what is.

Reality is simply what *is*. It follows rules of expediency, not rules of trust. And these rules of expediency aren't necessarily human. When the earth needs relief from a buildup of stress in its gut, it makes an earthquake. People die, but the larger entity, the earth, is duly relieved.

Narrowed to the human condition, the rule of expediency says, This individual, me, needs to survive, grow, and prosper. If this is inconvenient for someone else, that person is probably scheming to make things uncomfortable for me too. I'd better get there first.

I'm not trying to return here to the idea that war, and the international relations from which war generally springs, operates on rules of expediency. We've already discussed that. What I'm saying here is that the universe operates on rules of expediency. That's what makes it seem so unfriendly and hostile to human ideals and wishes. And what this means is that the human heart, in its natural state, contains within it this same law of expediency. We call that selfishness. But selfishness is contained even in our morality. That's the "animal desire" Mill was referring to.

So the spiritual interpretation of the gospel I've proposed may seem unsatisfactory, precisely because it doesn't seem to take into consideration all those jerks out there who ought to get their just punishment. But the problem with this dissatisfaction is that it rests on expediency, that animal desire which is sown into the standard human notion of justice.

Going beyond expediency, the spiritual interpretation seeks to solve the problem by removing the source of injustice from the human heart. This spiritual interpretation recognizes that if, to build a shelter of justice, you balance evil against evil (an eye for an eye), you get a house made of hate. That's the system of justice most of us dwell in.

In such a system of balancing one evil against another, calling one evil an offense and labeling the other a punishment, we build a community, or shelter, of trust using building blocks of evil. It works well enough in this world for the establishment of a civil community. People don't really have to love each other in such a community. They just have to trust each other.

Or do they? Lurking under the trust, is the ever-present will to do harm. In other words, evil, which is defined here as self-interest or expediency, lies at the heart even of civil society. Is it any wonder then that it shouldn't be found absent anywhere else?

War then is a mirror of what the world really is, civil society included. There's much wrongdoing and injustice in the best of societies, but these wrongs are hidden under a cloak of laws and customs emphasizing the importance of trust in human relations. So long as we believe in that bond of trust, believe that it works more often than it doesn't, civil harmony is more or less possible. But to a large extent it's an illusion. War shatters the illusion.

In war, whatever lies outside the needs of the military unit is a matter of expediency. Whatever lies inside is governed by trust. Since the dangers are so high, the bond of trust is of a purer form than is found in civil relations. And also, since the dangers are so high, expedient action will, when necessary, be taken without regard to the interests of what lies outside the military unit. Civilians caught in the middle will at times fall victim to the demands of expediency.

But again, this is what happens in civil society as well. The innocent are often unjustly punished, while the exploiting few continue to live undeservedly rich and more satisfying lives. That's because good and evil, generous trust and selfish expediency, are inside every individual, like the wheat and the chaff or the wheat and the tares.

We're creatures capable of humane ideals, but we live in a material universe without them. It's impossible to forget this. We never do. In the Christian New Testament letter to the Romans, the writer, Paul, says, "I see another law at work in the members of my body, waging war against the law of my mind." He's talking about the same thing.

As to the social level, Jesus put it another way in the Gospel of Mathew, "You will hear of wars and rumors of wars, but see to it that you are not alarmed. Such things must happen." That's because, if warfare between the ideal and the expedient is present in the human heart, it'll be expressed in the external, organized, and destructive sense of relations between men and societies as well.

I'm not pushing religion here, but I take useful insights where I find them. The literature of mankind, both religious and secular, is full of these insights, which have been gained at the cost of hard and painful experience. We should make use of them, if we want to understand ourselves and even begin to see why we do what we do.

Ordinary Men

Mark and I went on R and R at the same time. But I had only two months left to do in Vietnam and he had six or seven. We flew back from Hawaii in an airliner. Very nice. But all the way back he kept his face buried in a pillow set on a tray pulled down from the rear of the seat in front of him. He missed his wife and seemed to have the idea he would never see her again.

I managed to pick up a couple bottles of rum in Guam and one of them broke in my suitcase. Stunk like a distillery. We drank the other one the night we arrived in Vietnam. The roads were already closed so it was too late to get out to our unit. Mark got so blubbering drunk he slept in the middle of the floor of the hooch we were staying in for the night. And we both reeked from the rum, which we'd spilled down the front of our utility shirts. Some of the clerks in the hooch with us there at 1st Marine Division Headquarters thought Mark was strange. Not for the drinking but for the absolute abandon and sullen mood with which he did it. But I understood. After all, Darlene, his wife, whom I'd met, was a good looking woman. It's hard to go dry for six months after spending a week getting all wet again. Besides, the clerks thought I was strange too.

We were welcomed back to the battalion command post the next evening with a night of perimeter guard. The following day we would go out to our separate line companies.

Mark was a big blond Swedish looking guy. He was a little livelier that night. Vietnam kind of grows on you.

It was during my watch and his break that the Viet Cong hit us with one of their probing actions. It didn't amount to much. Just small

What Is War?

arms fire from across the river. But it got Mark up groggy and irritated. I think he was still half soused. And it kept us both awake.

The sergeant of the guard came by. He approached us in the dark without a flashlight, so as not to be picked off by the snipers. We guided him in with our voices, because we were on a knoll at the end of a finger of land extending out with steep mud banks from the main hill. The wire was down on part of it too, which was not supposed to be the case.

"Eighty-one mortar crew is going to get some illumination up," he said.

"Good. Can't see anything but the muzzle flashes."

"Nothing to worry about. It's just a probe and their angle of fire is too high to do much. Where you guys from?"

"Mike company," I said.

"Lima company," Mark said.

"I used to be with India. Too short now. I've got less than thirty days left in country."

Mark looked away toward the river and the muzzle flashes. The VC seemed to be shooting mostly at the main part of the perimeter. Mark and I were lying on top of the bunker, and Sgt. Hamner was crouching behind it because of the occasional whine of a bullet overhead. The bullets sounded like mosquitoes, and none of them were hitting anything. Then there was a dull thunk and a pop. The round white ball of a flare opened up above us and swung from its parachute. A little bit of movement could be seen in the village across the river. The air smelled damp and green, or even brown like the sluggish river water below us. Heavier fire was now being directed from our side, along the main perimeter, toward the Viet Cong. I squeezed off three rounds toward the movement I'd seen, but there was no return fire and I didn't see anything else.

"We had some LBGBs in the water a little earlier," the sergeant said.

"How many?"

"Six."

Tollefson

"What the hell's an LBGB?" Mark asked.

"Little bitty gook boat." Sgt. Hamner wasn't smiling, but I could see in the flat white glare of the flare light that the corners of his eyes were crinkled.

"Oh. So what happened to the sampans?"

"Nothing."

"Nothing?"

"Yeah. We thought they were going to cross the river toward our side, so we held fire to get a better look. But they didn't cross. The bridge guards who spotted them were disappointed."

"War's hell!"

"See you guys." The sergeant went off toward the next bunker.

There were a number of flares up now, and the shooting had stopped. The place was lit up like day and we had to contend with the metal canisters from the flares. They made a loud whistle coming down and put a pretty good dent into whatever they hit.

Mark started laughing, rolling over onto his back. "Ha ha ha."

"What's the matter?"

"Ha ha ha ha."

"Damn it, Mark, what's so funny?"

"Ha ha. Can't you see it? Ha ha ha. Tomorrow's headline in the *Stars and Stripes*: Marine killed by falling flare canister. Ha ha ha ha. Ha ha ha ha ha."

I remembered after we went back out to our separate companies, that Mark had told me he'd frozen once under fire. Frozen stiff and couldn't move. It had bothered him a lot, he said, until he realized it would never happen again.

And it didn't. The Marine Corps presented his wife and new born son with the Silver Star he earned.

* * *

Individual military acts of heroism can inspire men. Such acts encourage those who witness them to push on a little harder. That's why medals are awarded. They should be. Those medals, and the acts of valor that engender them, represent the highest virtues of courage and selflessness. Any institution, including the military, needs visible symbols like this to express its values, what it stands for. That's why countries have flags and war monuments. To give the people a sense of who they are and to provide them with a visible reminder of the sacrifices that have been made for them.

But it shouldn't be forgotten that the symbolism of the few is the reality of the many. Every day men and women in the armed forces make sacrifices. Yet there's no one to record or report every act. They are noble deeds, large and small, that go unsung. Without them the individual acts of the few who stand out would be meaningless. It's like a great poet who in a flash of genius reveals what many people have been struggling to express all along. It's their strength and effort he's gathered together and brought clarity to.

No one stands alone, and no extraordinary deed is without its ordinary support. Inscribed on the Iwo Jima memorial are the words, "Uncommon valor was a common virtue." Eugene Sledge, writing about the assault on Peleliu Island, expressed the opinion that more medals might've been handed out if so many hadn't been doing an outstanding job.

Courage, of course, isn't the exclusive domain of the military. It permeates life and human existence. It's the basis of the two highest virtues, truth and love. If ever there's to be a world without war, it'll be built upon courage and its twin offspring, truth and love. That's the supreme paradox, the one with which this book will end: Courage, which is given its boldest and purest expression in war, is the very thing which can bring an end to it. But it won't be a softhearted idealism that accomplishes this. It'll require a bold squaring with the facts.

It takes courage to look at life with an unflinching eye, to first of all remind oneself every day, as the French Renaissance essayist, Michel de Montaigne, expressed it, that all of life is a building of the house of death. Then, having accepted this, the day by day, moment by moment, reality of it, and to add onto it the further uncompromising awareness that we're continually attempting to deceive ourselves about our own motives—in other words, to face life squarely and honestly without once turning away from the burning reality of the true nature of our inner and outer lives, that's how we must begin. It's how the combatant is forced to deal with life. Let him teach us how to end war.

When we've done this and can develop the discipline to hold to it with faithfulness, we'll find our vision has changed. We'll discover a peace we hadn't thought possible before. Why is this? It's because, having faced down the demon of human limitation, having stood naked, as it were, before the universe, we can finally recognize and accept our proper place within it. A bold recognition of something is an acceptance of it. This acceptance is a form of letting go. It's the beginning of an end to struggle.

We can finally agree with Hemingway's old man:

> Imagine if each day a man must try to kill the moon, he thought. The moon runs away. But imagine if a man each day should have to try to kill the sun? We were born lucky, he thought.

We're born lucky because we only have to know and be what we are. Nothing else is required of us.

War itself is a product of anger and fear. When we seek to aggrandize ourselves, to expand our achievements at the expense of others, we're trying to alter our place in the natural order of things. This puts us into a grim struggle with our existence and with everyone who would block or oppose our progress. It also pits them against us. Out of this struggle comes an atmosphere of fear, of continual alarms and bitter retaliation. It's unfortunately the condition we normally call life, whether it be muted in civil appeasement or fully intoned in the aggression of war.

When I speak of the peace that's the antidote to this kind of continual unrest, I'm not looking for pie in the sky. I'm speaking practically. Love, which is the condition of this peace, isn't about intense affection and devotion. That's a private matter. It's always confined to a very few. Love in the larger sense is about respect.

When we can accept ourselves for what we really are and face our lives as we find them, we'll be able to allow others to do the same. This doesn't preclude any form of personal achievement which would ultimately benefit ourselves and others. It merely insists that that achievement should be an expression of what we are and not a theft from the potential of others.

Again, this is best illustrated in the place where it's least expected: on the battlefield. It seems that extreme ends bring us back to origins. War, the condition where fear and mutual struggle have broken into open hostility and mutual destruction, lays bare the essential nature of the problem of human fear, destructive ambition, and conflict. And this problem can only be met with courage, simplicity, and devotion. That's why young people are attracted to war. They're actually searching for its opposite.

Chapter Summary Questions

The Attraction of War
- Why does a young person go to war?
- What's meant by "the final boundaries of things" or "a confrontation with reality"?
- How does war provide "community of purpose in braving limitation"?

The Problem with Civilians
- How can it be said, "There's no ethical basis for war," while maintaining that "innocence *in any context* should be treated with humanity"?
- Are some feelings of empathy universal, such as maintaining that "the enjoyment of any suffering imposed upon the innocent is an abomination to all," or must the behavior of combatants only be judged in terms of their own nation's internal ethical standards?
- What's meant by "the exercise of cautious discipline"?

Morality as Military Discipline
- Why is trust the essential building block behind the three cardinal virtues of a military ground unit: discipline, esprit de corps, and unit integrity?
- How does the military moral bond differ from a civilian moral bond?
- Why is the physical and economic component of morality within a civil community inapplicable *in a moral sense* to a relationship between opposing forces?

The Complexity of Counterinsurgent Operations
- Given the use of coercion by insurgent forces, how easy is it to determine the degree of willing participation by a civilian when he or she is engaged in actions hostile to counterinsurgent forces?
- Is ethical behavior towards civilians tactically justified in terms of winning over the populace and therefore a matter of expedience in carrying out counterinsurgent operations?
- If a nation acts against its own stated principles in perpetrating war, how does this impact upon the moral consistency of its own people?

The Quality of Troops
- How can the "moral dilemma" of assault troops assigned to counterinsurgent operations against guerilla forces be characterized?
- How might constraint under duress be understood to define military discipline?
- How might it define discipline in a civil context?

Combat Deaths
- What is it we fear to lose when we say we fear death?
- What does it mean to say that life is limitation?
- What inner conflict is it that makes a combatant more "knowing" than most other people?

The Rhythms of Conflict
- If courage stands midway between cowardice, on the one hand, and both bravery and bravado, on the other, how do bravery and bravado differ?
- Considered as a universal condition, how is war characteristic of the world in general?
- Is peace in the human heart achieved under different internal circumstances than physical peace in the outer world?

Tollefson

Guerrilla Versus Counterinsurgent Operations
- What makes guerilla campaigns against superior forces possible?
- What kinds of psychological and social conditions can cause foreign troops to become overbearing in attitude?
- How should civilians be treated, given the treachery of some of them, especially when the dangerous and unreliable portion of the population is hard to identify?

The Moral Uncertainty of War
- As compared to the United States, how is Mexico's slow social and economic development to be explained?
- How does a foreign power determine the comparative legitimacy of opposing claims to sovereignty in another country?
- If civilians are unwillingly or unknowingly aiding the enemy, how should they be treated?

The Socialization of Combat
- Describing sympathy as an emotional capacity and empathy as an imaginative capacity involving sympathy, what is empathy?
- How is the exercise of the social instinct qualified, or limited, in a combatant?
- Are combatants and politicians accountable for wars in the same ways?

War as a Reflection of Life
- What does it mean to say that life is actually experienced "whole and complete"?
- While the specific nature of laws regulating the degree and manner of punishment of a criminal falls within the moral sphere, the *execution* of that punishment does not. Why is this?
- Within a moral context, can a person express sincerity while finding it expedient for the purpose of self-protection to deceive another concerning the facts about himself?

What Is War?

The Right of Military Interference
- What constitutes a legitimate right of interference of one country in another country's affairs?
- What accounts for the self-defensive posture of nations toward one another, and why does this posture imply a complete abrogation of moral principles?
- If there's no such thing as a moral war, how can practical considerations of the suffering that might be caused by a proposed war be relevant?

The Social Responsibility of Warring Nations
- Why should a nation always openly receive its veterans home, treating them as a part of itself?
- What is in us that makes us unwilling to let go of the idea that some part of us should be exempt from death?
- What do both the inevitability of death and our unavoidable tendency to make mistakes have in common as fundamental characteristics of human existence?

Discipline as a Military Virtue
- What does it mean to say that an effective military unit is a "close-meshed structure, forged in discipline and held together by esprit"?
- How did the lieutenant in the vignette put himself in the no man's land of expedience, which cost him his life?
- Are soldiers entirely free of the laws of the civil community they leave behind?

The Fabrication of Wars
- How much influence does an American have over the war-making powers of his government?
- Does popularizing the delivery of news (by responding to ratings) affect the quality of its presentation?

- How can a people who call themselves free be considered both responsible and not responsible for their nation's wars?

How War Defines Being
- What does it mean to say that we're human *because* we're part of the human group?
- Explain why our experience of both nature and God is to be found in consciousness alone.
- Why can it be said that life in essence is nothing more than an expression of simple existence and community, and how does this relate to a young person's desire to experience war?

The Demands of War
- How might battlefield conditions complicate the moral accountability of combatants?
- Held against the standards of a civilized community, are battlefield decisions and acts mitigated in some way?
- How might public opinion effect the decisions of a military tribunal concerning an "unlawful" act in war?

The Many Historical Causes of War
- What's the meaning of the phrase, "War, like refined sugar, is made because the canes stand ripe in the field and ready for harvest," and what factors contribute to this?
- If "history is a dizzying myriad of forces all acting simultaneously," how does one account for events with any degree of certainty?
- In the interest of ending war, how might the human heart be given a peaceful, honest, and fulfilling direction?

Finding Purpose in the Military
- What does it mean to say "there's no evidence of a specific thing called will"?
- In terms of our sense of self-definition, what's the appeal of a well-defined group, especially the military?

- Do men follow leaders or the charisma of the groups they symbolize?

The Ruthlessness of War
- When do the ends justify the means in warfare, and when don't they?
- What accounts for varying levels of empathy in and out of warfare?
- How do shifts in personal identity and the presence or removal of a threat affect a person's capacity for empathy?

Military Power
- How might our need for others to be *conscious of us* cause conflict?
- Explain why it is that the four principal forms of war—insurrection, invasion, a struggle over resources, and a struggle over spheres of influence—are inevitably intermixed.
- How does egoism lie at the political heart of war?

A Veteran in Society
- How does war "cleanse the soul"?
- What differentiates the war experience from an earthquake or a tsunami, and why is this so?
- How can a breakdown of individual character, confidence, and trust occur in and result from a society which refuses to accept its own complicity in the act of making war?

Good Logistics and Spiritual Fortitude
- If "values are what a stout heart clings to when all else fails," what values should a combatant have?
- How is faith "a relationship between a person and his or her existence"?
- How does faith in values *create* strong character and purpose? Relate this to the stress of combat.

Tollefson

Casualties of War
- What is meant by the term "divided soul"?
- How can it be said that a system of justice is built upon hate?
- In what way can it be said that warfare between the ideal and the expedient is in every human endeavor?

Ordinary Men
- What is the paradox with which this book ends?
- In what way can the combatant teach us how to end war?
- What is the "essential nature" of the problem of human fear, destructive ambition, and conflict?

Sources and Recommended Reading

Alexander, Joseph H. *A Fellowship of Valor: The Battle History of the United States Marines.* Read by Richard M. Davidson. Audiocassette. Recorded Books, 1998.

Aristotle. "Nicomachean Ethics." Trans. W. D. Ross. *Great Books of the Western World.* Ed. Robert Maynard Hutchins. Vol. 9. Chicago: Encyclopedia Britannica, 1952.

---. "Politics." Trans. Benjamin Jowett. *Great Books of the Western World.* Ed. Robert Maynard Hutchins. Vol. 9. Chicago: Encyclopedia Britannica, 1952.

Beauvoir, Simone de. *The Ethics of Ambiguity.* Trans. Bernard Frechtman. New York: Philosophical Library, 1949.

Caesar, Julius. *The Conquest Of Gaul.* Trans. S. A. Handford. Baltimore: Penguin Books, 1958.

"The Constitution of the United States of America." *Great Books of the Western World.* Ed. Robert Maynard Hutchins. Vol. 43. Chicago: Encyclopedia Britannica, 1952.

Crane, Stephen. "The Red Badge of Courage." *Four American Novels.* New York: Harcourt, Brace and World, 1959.

Donne, John. "Meditation XVII." *The Norton Anthology of English Literature.* Ed. M. H. Abrams. Vol. 1. New York: Norton, 1974.

Guevara, Che. *Guerilla Warfare.* Trans. J. P. Morray. New York: Vintage Books, 1961.

Hegel, Georg Wilhelm Friedrich. "The Philosophy of History." Trans. J. Sibree. *Great Books of the Western World.* Ed. Robert Maynard Hutchins. Vol. 46. Chicago: Encyclopedia Britannica, 1952.

Hemingway, Ernest. *Ernest Hemingway on Writing.* Ed. Larry W. Phillips. New York: Charles Scribner's Sons, 1984.

---. *The Old Man and the Sea.* New York: Charles Scribner's Sons, 1952.

---. "Soldier's Home." *The Complete Short Stories of Ernest Hemingway.* New York: Charles Scribner's Sons, 1987.

Hobbes, Thomas. "Leviathan, Or, Matter, Form, and Power of a Commonwealth, Ecclesiastical and Civil." *Great Books of the Western World.* Ed. Robert Maynard Hutchins. Vol. 23. Chicago: Encyclopedia Britannica, 1952.

The Holy Bible: King James Version. New York: Collins' Cleartype Press, 1949.

Hopkins, William B. *One Bugle No Drums: The Marines at the Chosin Reservoir.* Chapel Hill: Algonquin Books, 1986.

Jefferson, Thomas. "The Declaration of Independence." *Great Books of the Western World.* Ed. Robert Maynard Hutchins. Vol. 43. Chicago: Encyclopedia Britannica, 1952.

Kant, Immanuel. "Fundamental Principles of the Metaphysic of Morals." Trans. Thomas Kingsmill Abbott. *Great Books of the Western World.* Ed. Robert Maynard Hutchins. Vol. 42. Chicago: Encyclopedia Britannica, 1952.

---. "General Introduction to the Metaphysic of Morals." Trans. W. Hastie. *Great Books of the Western World.* Ed. Robert Maynard Hutchins. Vol. 42. Chicago: Encyclopedia Britannica, 1952.

Karnow, Stanley. *Vietnam: A History.* New York: Viking Press, 1983.

Kline, Morris. *Mathematics and the Search for Knowledge.* New York: Oxford University Press, 1986.

Locke, John. "Concerning Civil Government, Second Essay." *Great Books of the Western World.* Ed. Robert Maynard Hutchins. Vol. 35. Chicago: Encyclopedia Britannica, 1952.

Machiavelli, Niccolò. "The Prince." Trans. W. K. Marriott. *Great Books of the Western World.* Ed. Robert Maynard Hutchins. Vol. 23. Chicago: Encyclopedia Britannica, 1952.

Marx, Karl and Friedrich Engels. "Manifesto of the Communist Party." Trans. Samuel Moore. *Great Books of the Western World.* Ed. Robert Maynard Hutchins. Vol. 50. Chicago: Encyclopedia Britannica, 1952.

Mill, John Stuart. "Utilitarianism." *Great Books of the Western World.* Ed. Robert Maynard Hutchins. Vol. 43. Chicago: Encyclopedia Britannica, 1952.

Montaigne, Michel de. "The Essays of Michel Eyquem de Montaigne." Trans. Charles Cotton. *Great Books of the Western World.* Ed. Robert Maynard Hutchins. Vol. 25. Chicago: Encyclopedia Britannica, 1952.

The New International Version Bilingual New Testament, Psalms and Proverbs (Spanish/English). Grand Rapids: Zondervan, 1999.

Nietzsche, Friedrich. *Beyond Good and Evil.* Trans. Walter Kaufmann. New York: Vintage Books, 1989.

Plato. "The Dialogues of Plato." Trans. Benjamin Jowett. *Great Books of the Western World.* Ed. Robert Maynard Hutchins. Vol. 7. Chicago: Encyclopedia Britannica, 1952.

Plutarch. "The Lives of the Noble Grecians and Romans." Trans. Dryden et al. *Great Books of the Western World.* Ed. Robert Maynard Hutchins. Vol. 14. Chicago: Encyclopedia Britannica, 1952.

Remarque, Erich Maria. *All Quiet on the Western Front.* Trans. A. W. Wheen. New York: Fawcett, 1981.

Russ, Martin. Breakout: The Chosin Reservoir Campaign, Korea 1950. New York: Fromm International, 1999.

Sledge, E. B. *With the Old Breed: At Peleliu and Okinawa.* Annapolis: Naval Institute Press, 1996.

Smith, Huston. The World's Religions: Our Great Wisdom Traditions. San Francisco: Harper, 1991.

Tolstoy, Leo. "War and Peace." Trans. Louise and Aylmer Maude. *Great Books of the Western World.* Ed. Robert Maynard Hutchins. Vol. 51. Chicago: Encyclopedia Britannica, 1952.

Tucker, Spencer C., ed. Encyclopedia of The Vietnam War: A Political, Social, and Military History. New York: Oxford University Press, 2000.

Xenophon. *The Persian Expedition.* Trans. Rex Warner. New York: Penguin Books, 1979.

www.ingramcontent.com/pod-product-compliance
Lightning Source LLC
Chambersburg PA
CBHW070425010526
44118CB00014B/1900